British Choral Music
nineteenth & twentieth century music
for choral societies

LEWIS FOREMAN: books and theses on music

Havergal Brian: a collection of essays (1969)
The British Musical Renaissance (1972)
Discographies: a bibliography (1973)
Archive Sound Collections (1974)
Systematic Discography (1974)
Factors Affecting the Preservation and Dissemination of Archive Sound Recordings (1975)
British Music Now (1975)
Havergal Brian and the Performance of his Orchestral Music (1976)
Edmund Rubbra: composer (1977)
Dermot O'Byrne: poems by Arnold Bax (1979)
Arthur Bliss: catalogue of the complete works (1980)
The Percy Grainger Companion (1981)
Bax: a composer and his times (1983; 2nd ed 1988; 3rd ed in preparation)
Oskar Fried: Delius and the late romantic school (1984)
From Parry to Britten: British music in letters (1987, 1988)
Farewell, My Youth and other writings by Sir Arnold Bax (1992)
Lost and Only Sometimes Found: a seminar on music publishing and archives (1992)
British Music 1885-1921 (1994)
*Koanga: the 1935 production of Frederick Delius's opera in the context of its
    performance history* (1995)
Vaughan Williams in Perspective (1998)
Elgar & Gerontius: the early performances (1998)

FRONTISPIECE [OVERLEAF]
Sir Arthur Sullivan:
a Victorian engraving after
a photograph by
Devereux, Brighton.

Arthur Sullivan

A BRITISH MUSIC SOCIETY PUBLICATION

British Choral Music
a Millennium performing conspectus
of nineteenth & twentieth century music
for choral societies

Celebrating performances
given by the competing choral societies
in the British Music Society
Millennium Choral Competition
2000-2001

EDITED BY LEWIS FOREMAN

British Music Society
2001

ISBN: 1 870536 21 5

Published by the British Music Society,
7 Tudor Gardens, Upminster, Essex RM14 3DE

Copies are available price £8.95 post free

British Library Cataloguing in Publication Data
A CIP record for this book is available from the British Library

Printed by The Arc & Throstle Press Ltd
Nanholme Mill, Shaw Wood Road, Todmorden, Lancs OL14 6DA

First published 2001

Contents

Illustrations

1. INTRODUCTION

THE BRITISH MUSIC SOCIETY & THE CHORAL COMPETITION FOR THE MILLENNIUM

RAPHAEL TERRONI
Chairman, British Music Society

IN 1985 THE BRITISH MUSIC SOCIETY (BMS) RAN A COMPETITION for amateur operatic companies to present operas by British composers. Since then there have been successful competitions for singers and players of various instruments including piano, woodwind, strings and organ. However, not since the inaugural Opera Awards in 1985 has the BMS undertaken such an ambitious enterprise as the Choral Competition for the Millennium. British choral music has a proud tradition that stretches back many centuries and as we have seen during the course of this choral celebration it is still as strong as ever.

With the help of Lewis Foreman's list of suggested repertoire (see p 106) intrepid choirs took the plunge into uncharted territory and without exception successfully met our challenge. It was gratifying to see the fruition of an idea that I had had some years ago and had been considered in committee to be too ambitious at that time and quite rightly so. I must therefore make special mention of those who have now made this idea a reality. Lewis Foreman acted as our adviser and has produced this volume. He also spent many hours copying instrumental parts and supplying programme notes with seemingly boundless energy. I thank the BMS committee and especially our previous chairman John Talbot who steered the project through all the vital stages. As with all the BMS Awards Stan Meares has masterminded this event with military precision. No detail was overlooked and it would be fair to say that the Competition could not have taken place without his enormous contribution. John Alldis our distinguished chairman of the Jury guided the panel with great charm and wisdom. We thank him and the other judges most sincerely for their hard work.

Our special thanks to the RVW Trust for so generously supporting this project. The sheer scale of this competition required the help of outside funding. Without this support it would not have been possible.

Needless to say, most of all we thank the choral societies who participated. In every instance audiences were given memorable performances. We very much appreciate all the hard work that they, their orchestras, soloists and conductors put into the preparation of these concerts. Through their enterprise some fine choral works were given an all too rare airing. To say that they are all masterpieces would be foolish but amongst them we did hear pieces that ought to feature more often in the programmes of choral societies throughout the land.

To the winners of the first prize of £2,500, the Savoyard Chorus of Edinburgh and their conductor David Lyle, and the winner of the second prize of £1,000, the Guildford Choral Society conducted by Hilary Davan Wetton our warm congratulations.

The judges also awarded two discretionary prizes. Firstly, for enterprise, to the Birmingham Festival Choral Society conducted by Anthony Bradbury and Jeremy Patterson. Their remarkable programme juxtaposing a revival from 1930, the *Requiem* by Frédéric d'Erlanger, with a vibrant score by a living composer, *For the Beauty of the Earth* by John Joubert, required an enormous amount of research and preparation and emphasised that this was a competition for living music. Secondly, for communication, to the Milton Keynes Chorale, in recognition of conductor John Gibbons' personal presentation of a technically difficult programme (Joubert again) which he made notably accessible for the general listener.

The judges attended twelve concerts up and down the country, which were all so unfailingly interesting and enjoyable that it is a pity that there had to be winners, for there certainly were no losers. Everyone acquitted themselves well and every event was memorable. Congratulations to all.

2. BRITISH CHOIRS & BRITISH MUSIC

JOHN ALLDIS
Chairman of the Judges, Millennium Choral Competition

OVER A PERIOD OF MORE THAN SIX MONTHS THE JUDGES OF THE British Music Society's Millennium Choral Competition crossed and re-crossed the country hearing local choral societies presenting programmes which included a variety of revivals of music written by British composers over the century and a quarter from the 1870s to today. I was delighted to have been asked to participate in this exercise which presented me with a range of works I had not previously heard. It was always stimulating and included several interesting finds. It also gave one a perspective on choral society activity from Edinburgh to Guildford and from Hereford to Sheffield.

As the chairman of the judges may I say that it was a pleasure to see so much evidence of a still living and widely practised tradition, if with one or two worrying signs of future problems of which the most notable was certainly the rising average age of both singers and audiences, though how refreshing to see so many youthful faces in the orchestras.

And what of the repertoire chosen by the choirs? Much of it came new to me, and I was particularly impressed by Sullivan and by Dyson, whose *Agincourt* was the only work to be offered by two competitors. How good, too, to see so many competitors offering music by living composers, half a dozen or so written in the last few years. For me, possibly overall Christopher Brown's only recently composed *Invocation* was the most rewarding discovery, and I commend it to others, while the 'Canticle of the Birds' an extract from Richard Blackford's St Francis of Assisi cantata *Mirror of Perfection* that we heard at Bury St Edmunds, was delightful: music that really communicated. Blackford's setting has the added advantage that readers can easily investigate it for themselves, as there is a commercial recording.

The contrast with what one might experience in Europe was as ever instructive. First the clear evidence of a widespread and very active British choral tradition which generally addresses a long tradition of native composition was both heartening and disheartening. Our long-practised ability to get a performance together with only one orchestralrehearsal is probably the principal determinant of the standards achieved. The performances – except perhaps that heard at Cambridge – all exemplified the British choral society practice of a gradient of slowly improving rehearsals, often over several months, crowned by the performance given at the peak – a procedure requiring considerable experience to judge that the peak comes at the right moment. The alternative, a shorter period of preparation is more dependent on sheer technique, but can well make for a fresher effect at the performance.

Overall – and I speak with 40 years practical experience – my feeling was reinforced that at the end of the day the man (unfortunately we were presented with no women conductors) out front is responsible for what ensues. It is the conductor who enables his performers to seek the 'now', the 'moment', imposing nothing which fails to help him reveal the meaning behind the text. This is the ingredient which makes a performance different, and it happened several times during the competition. But to become really special, every member of the choir needs to become even more professional in intention, never to relax between moments, but to concentrate on the need to give a 'performance'. This is something that comes from within, so that everybody is in a sense a soloist. Our choral practice tends to be corporate, to coo, and to back off.

Repertoire creates standards and needs to be demanding. In my view generally choral repertoire is chosen from a limited list of long-standing favourites, which is why a competition to present revivals was such a good idea. Eventually we become damaged by repetition and ultimately it becomes boring only to do the things that are loved. This also relates to the renewal of the whole choral society movement: recruiting young people has implications for the repertoire, playing their repertoire stimulates both choirs and audiences.

I hope all involved in the competition enjoyed the experience, and took away aspirations for the future – they certainly all seemed to attract audiences, the usual reason for committees not wanting to move into fresh pastures. It was a healthy sign, too, to find that as well as such worthwhile revivals as Sullivan without Gilbert and the less well-known works of Parry we heard a number of notable works by living composers. So I would encourage all involved to widen their repertoire

During the competition, the music was generally experienced in resonant halls, often themselves very beautiful in terms of architecture, texture and colour, and part of the experience. And in almost every example this is music that was written to exist in a big space. In some cases the choice of repertoire and location were complementary, while in a few they were not so happy, particularly where the acoustic prevented the words from coming across.

It would be invidious to write in specific terms, but generally a positive impression was received of choral discipline. Voices were reasonably well-balanced though the shortage of tenors was in evidence in almost every choir. Choirs were all able to make a big sound, they were less sure in quiet moments, due to a lack of vocal technique which is *never* insoluble with practice. One had more reservations about diction – when the words could be understood it added notably to the effect of the performances. Tuning, too, can become a problem though it was acceptable in most cases. Perhaps more critical is rhythmic diction, intensity and blend.

We are not adjudicating on the achievement of the soloists that were offered. This is a notable field in which young singers gain professional experience on the choral society circuit, and here they had to sing many works which they will probably not frequently encounter again. Here I should say that the judges neither advanced nor rejected any performance owing to problems with soloists, but as well as one or two very promising names, we did experience one or two where the soloists, at least in passing, rather let down otherwise commendable enterprises.

Speaking for the British Music Society and its panel of judges I must thank those choral societies who participated. All these choirs showed enterprise and joined in the spirit of the competition; it would have been diminished by the loss of any of them. Together they made the whole exercise a worthwhile one.

It was interesting to note that during the period of the competition a number of other choirs offered programmes of British music which would have been very competitive had they entered. While regretting that they did not participate, it was also good to see that the competition represents a living tradition on the part of many choral societies and that it is in no way a specialised local interest.

Chorus and Orchestra of Edinburgh and their conductor David Lyle who won the first prize, and the Guildford Choral Society and their conductor Hilary Davan Wetton who won the second prize. Secondly the two winners of the judges' discretionary prizes: the Birmingham Festival Choral Society and its conductors Anthony Bradbury and Jeremy Patterson and the Milton Keynes Chorale and its conductor John Gibbons. I must also thank the British Music Society and my fellow judges Lewis Foreman, Stan Meares, Malcolm

Smith, John Talbot and Raphael Terroni.

This publication is intended to be a practical guide based on the experience of the performances prepared and given throughout the period of the competition. It gives the background, programme notes and sources for the works performed. I commend this exploratory frame of mind and I hope it excites all choral society directors and their committees to broaden their repertoire. There is so huge a literature for choral societies that there is no need constantly to perform the same few works. A wider repertoire of itself surely creates higher standards, and by developing the range of works offered and raising these standards we are contributing to developing the next generation of choral singers and keeping it a living music.

3. LIVING MUSIC
the British choral heritage in performance

LEWIS FOREMAN

THE SECOND HALF OF THE NINETEENTH CENTURY IN THE UNITED KINGDOM saw the choral festival movement provide a regular opportunity for the presentation of new music to a public that supported it. These overlapping cycles of festivals up and down the country meant that there were at least one or two such occasions every year, and they almost always featured new music, combined with the inevitable favourites of *Messiah* and *Elijah*. Many of these festivals ended with the First World War, although after the war the Three Choirs and the Norwich Festival, in particular, continued. However, by 1919 the aesthetic had completely changed and Victorian composers were rejected – 'those ghastly dullards' Bax called them. In fact he was wrong to make such a wide-sweeping generalisation, but it took several generations to discover that.

The inter-war period itself was a time of remarkable choral composition, not on the previous scale, but it saw the emergence of Bliss, Ferguson, Foulds, Hadley, Lambert, Moeran and Walton among many other leading names who have not been heard during the British Music Society's Millennium Choral Competition and so are not further discussed here. But all wrote major choral works and all are worth investigation. In effect the later established twentieth century repertoire was almost all written in the first half of the century. By this time Vaughan Williams was the dominant force, and in a repertoire which once established has continued to the present day.

The competition had the objective of providing an opportunity to review British choral music written over the last hundred and fifty years in performance, and in particular to explore those seemingly worthwhile works which deserved a hearing but had been forgotten. The competition ran from September 2000 to April 2001, and, in the view of those who participated, it triumphantly demonstrated that there is much unknown worthwhile repertoire for local choral societies to explore. For this writer at least, every competing choral society's discoveries were good to hear, one or two coming with the force of a revelation. For this was no dry as dust picking over of antiquarian survivals, but memorable, living music – it is difficult to know quite why it had been forgotten. At the beginning of a new Millennium the choirs surely let us hear that this is a repertoire worthy of investigation in performance, and that the history of British music of the period needs actively revisiting in the light of such live performances. Here is a worthwhile tradition that deserves to live, and is within the capabilities of most choral societies up and down the country. In twelve concerts we only heard some thirty choral works, about half of them complete revivals. But there could be no doubt that it is the tip of a musical iceberg; there remains a large, and largely uncharted, worthwhile repertoire still worth exploring.

In the event twelve short-listed choirs presented vibrant performances of thirty works written between 1872 and 2001. These were all in themselves enjoyable, and in addition a number of remarkable discoveries were made that could be investigated by other choral societies planning future seasons – and should certainly be on the list for record companies looking for attractive new repertoire to explore. This essay surveys the music in chronological order of composition and sets it in its historical context. For more detail, read the programme notes for each revival which have been reprinted from the programmes of the competing concerts. We are most grateful to the choirs and authors concerned for their permission to reproduce them here.

Generally British choral music of the second half of the nineteenth century had a bad press in the twentieth century, and for decades it was little played. Apart from the huge success of Mendelssohn's *Elijah*, first heard at the Birmingham Festival of 1846, possibly the earliest music still widely heard has been *Blest Pair of Sirens* of 1887, in retrospect a forward-looking score for its time. Alone it has never been displaced as a much loved self-evident masterpiece of the period. Hearing it again in the atmospheric acoustic of St James's Cathedral, Bury St Edmunds, under the baton of Harrison Oxley, was to be reminded on how many levels it has remained a cornerstone of the British choral repertoire, an imperishable monument of its period and a favourite with choirs despite running less than eleven minutes.

It was to Sullivan we had to look for examples of the staple repertoire of the Victorian choral festival: the extended choral work, though in the case of the competition no one revived a full-blown oratorio. But in the Sullivan centenary year it was good to be reminded of Sullivan without Gilbert, and in two striking scores which have not been widely heard nor had a good press after their initial celebrity. The earliest was Sullivan's *Te Deum Laudamus 'Domine salvam fac reginam'* of 1872, written in thanksgiving for the recovery of the future King Edward VII from typhoid, and making a celebratory close to Ronald Corp's nicely judged programme with the Highgate Choral Society. There is no need to turn up one's nose at the uproarious finale – this is a delightful score showing its composer's fingerprints throughout. It is perhaps worth mentioning a practical point: here the seemingly innocent-looking solo soprano part requires an artist of stature to do justice to its soaring lines. This was true of many of the works heard, and many solo artists, some professional, some amateur, added to the pleasure of attending the competing performances.

Invidious perhaps to mention individual soloists in a competition for choral societies, but as a personal choice I particularly enjoyed the performances of Christine Rice, mezzo soprano, at Guildford, and Alan Fairs, the bass-baritone at Birmingham. Viewed chronologically, the *Te Deum Laudamus* was followed by what proved to be our competition winner, Sullivan's *The Golden Legend*, a great hit at the Leeds Festival in 1886, after which it was one of the most sung of all extended British choral works for some 15 or 20 years, but was already largely forgotten after the First World War. This is a gorgeous score and despite the somewhat creaky story Sullivan's music carries all before it. It made a very worthwhile winner as a piece as well as a performance.

There are many worthwhile choral works by Sir Charles Villiers Stanford still awaiting revival. We had Stanford's *Ave Atque Vale* of 1909, which, in fact, could have been written any time in the preceding thirty years. No one associated with the competition had heard it before, and as so often, while a piano run-through gave an approximate idea of its appeal, a hearing with the orchestra proved to be necessary before it could be fully appreciated. The concept of a choral overture is an original one, and it was good to add this to one's repertoire of occasional works suitable to open a concert or be used on a memorial occasion. Although Stanford incorporates 'Glorious things of Thee are spoken' (Haydn's *Austrian Hymn*) he does so with a remarkably light hand and apart from the bombastic closing bars this was a welcome revival: a typical occasional work by its composer, beautifully turned.

For those in thrall to the British choral music of the Elgarian period, the music written between the first performance of Elgar's *The Dream of Gerontius* in 1900 and the outbreak of war on 4 August 1914, encompasses a remarkable number of high points, including as it does not only Elgar's two big oratorios, but also Vaughan Williams's *A Sea Symphony*, many of Delius's major choral works and Bantock's *Omar Khayyám*. It was a time when strong new voices were beginning to appear, and three works from this time were programmed, all indicative of the musical and spiritual quest being forged by their composers. Two were well-known, but the quite unknown choral symphony *Before Sunrise* of

1907 by the 27 year-old Edgar Bainton, though not published or performed until after the First World War, came in Robert Tucker's performance with the Broadheath Singers at Eton College, as a striking example of the ambition of a new generation to say something new. It was Bainton's bad luck to find himself in competition with some of the most original and demanding new choral works of the new century. As it is he produced a first movement, 'Genesis', which may yet find itself a place in the repertoire as an independent orchestral work, some glorious and memorable choral writing, but with a sectional finale which needs very careful handling to weld it into a convincing whole. Beside Vaughan Williams's *A Sea Symphony* it is a less convincing work. Much better-known, and from the same period came Vaughan Williams's *Toward the Unknown Region* and Delius's *Songs of Sunset* both clearly establishing their composers' personal voices and both works that have lasted. The Broadheath Singers' presentation of the Delius was notable for its provision of the composer's call for various extras, not always heard even on professional recordings, including heckelphone, the bass or baritone oboe of which conductor Robert Tucker remarked 'it is such an important part and having the authentic sound was doubly wonderful'. Even more interesting was the metallic sound of the contra-bass sarrusophone, a part often heard on contrabassoon, but here reminding us of the demands of its period for orchestral colour and ever widening musical sensation.

From 1912 came three glorious works, one, Elgar's *The Music Makers*, familiar in choral society programmes, but the others very rarely heard and they proved worthwhile revivals indeed. Strangely both are Christmas pieces: Parry's wide-spanning *Ode on the Nativity* revived by Dr Roy Massey at Hereford, and Benjamin Dale's more compact *Before the Paling of the Stars* given by Ronald Corp with the Highgate Choral Society. Here we have two comparatively short settings (25 and 16 minutes respectively) and both curiously touching, Parry's late setting of Dunbar sublimating a lifetime's experience of choral music in a gentle but unexpectedly powerful vision. Many commentators have thought it possibly to be Parry's masterpiece and on this showing it must certainly rank with his best half-dozen scores.

If with Parry and Dale we have two scores which are eminently worthy of investigation by choral societies everywhere, even more so are two very touching works from the First World War. Both of them short, yet both deeply felt. Parry's *The Chivalry of the Sea* of 1916 was written in the face of a specific naval disaster and loss, which the composer sublimated in universal terms. It packed a big punch for a fourteen-minute piece, and was, as always with Parry, grateful to sing. It would find a ready place in many choral society programmes – as a curtain raiser to *Gerontius* or *A Sea Symphony* – or in its own right in a more modest presentation. In contrast Frank Bridge's more muted *A Prayer* was written in 1916 but was not heard during the war. Bridge's grief was more private and all-encompassing, his music a hymn to peace, but again he produced a striking work which has the added incentive for choral societies that the Frank Bridge Trust might well provide some financial support for a performance.

The works offered for the competition covered most of the big names of the early twentieth century, perhaps the most important omission being Gustav Holst, whose *The Hymn of Jesus* was, in 1920, not only the most widely welcomed new work in its day, but was a significant harbinger of modernism in British music after the First World War. We did not have Holst, but we did have Holst's friend William Gillies Whittaker, whose choral setting of William Habington's mystical poem *Cœlestial Spheares*, of 1923, might well be considered 'school' of Holst. Although nearly eighty years old, this is still a difficult work for both audiences and singers alike, perhaps looking forward to Holst's pupil Edmund Rubbra whose similar ecstatic vision, in his *Song of the Soul*, dates from almost thirty years later.

Whittaker's Holstian austerity, his 'fire and ice', could not be in greater contrast to the remarkable revival of Frédéric d'Erlanger's gorgeous – one reviewer called it ' gooey' – *Messe de Requiem* of 1931. Some professed to find it too sweet but any choir that has enjoyed Puccini's *Gloria* or Gounod's *St Cecilia Mass*, might find this worth exploring. D'Erlanger did not study in the UK, and with his French training he looked to the giants of Italian and French choral music for his language and produced a populist quasi-operatic setting that only needs repetition for it to be taken to heart. Previously the non-availability of performing materials was a major barrier to performance, but with vocal scores and orchestral parts having been produced for its revival at Birmingham, it is again easily available. The strong writing for the soloists and the glorious welling climaxes proclaim an operatic composer, and indeed the tenor's *appassionato* solo at 'Quam olim Abrahae promisisti' actually quotes from d'Erlanger's opera *Tess*, his setting of Hardy's *Tess of the d'Urbevilles*. The two lollipops for treble soloist 'Pie Jesu' and 'Requiem Aeternam' are an additional inducement for a choir wanting to give an opportunity to a really strong treble.

From the same date, but notably different in idiom was another quite individual voice that had also been forgotten. This was George Oldroyd, sometime Professor of Music at London University. His haunting setting of *Jhesu Christ, St Mary's Sone* of 1931, revived by Harrison Oxley at Bury St Edmunds, came as completely new to most of those present.

This 26-minute work, setting the fourteenth century Yorkshire mystic Richard Rolle of Hampole, almost all of it slow, did not seem a great prospect on the basis of the vocal score. But in performance it proved a magical and original musical canvas, a triumph for Harrison Oxley's performers at Bury. The choral writing is relatively simple – Oldroyd took plainsong tunes and set them, often in unison or two parts, against a gorgeous romantic orchestral texture – providing incandescent climaxes and treasurable reflective moments. Some took against it, perhaps sensing from Oldroyd's subtitle 'a spiritual rhapsody', that it is a backward-looking work. But for this listener, at least, this is far from the truth: with its plainsong-derived treatment of the vocal lines it finds a remarkable unity with the new simplicity of the music of seventy years on. This is a work which if it has been sung at all, has undoubtedly been done with organ – yet it needed the rich kaleidoscope of the orchestra as a setting for the chorus. Certainly the reviewer on the *East Anglian Daily Times* (19 March 2001) was moved by it, writing: 'This is a marvellous work, bound to plainsong so reinvented it could have been composed yesterday . . . And all sung by a choir that was wholly understanding of the text, comfortable in the idiom and communicative of the music.'

Oldroyd wrote for local performers, in his case at Croydon Parish Church in the 1930s. A dozen years later and in the darkest days of the war, Walter Hussey, later Dean of Chichester, at St Matthew's Northampton initiated a remarkable creative outpouring in the arts, starting with commissions to mark the fiftieth anniversary of the consecration of the church in 1943. This quickly attracted national celebrity for the leading names that were involved. Notably Henry Moore's 'Madonna and Child' which, unveiled in 1944, attracted an outcry for its perceived modernism. During our competition the first three Northampton musical commissions were heard, reminding us of Walter Hussey's sure musical instinct. Possibly the most familiar is Britten's *Rejoice in the Lamb*, settings of words by Christopher Smart from 1943. In 1945 came Lennox Berkeley's big-boned *Festival Anthem*, perhaps the least familiar, and it was good to hear it again. Third was the commission for 1946, Gerald Finzi *Lo the Full Final Sacrifice*, reminding us, if a reminder was needed, of Finzi's wonderful sympathy for voices and choral textures.

St Matthew's Northampton brings us conveniently to the next

unexpected revival in the competition, Christopher Le Fleming's *Five Psalms*. In the 1960s Le Fleming's Communion Service in D was commissioned for St Matthew's reminding us of an all-round practical composer who has been all but forgotten since his death in 1985. First heard at the 1945 Three Choirs, Le Fleming's unpretentious *Five Psalms* was less than warmly received, on account of its perceived lack of what then counted for modernism. However, its performance by the Sheffield Oratorio Choir conducted by Alan Eost was of a work in their repertoire and their third performance in ten years. This is practical and effective music, particularly useful for a choir seeking to use a small orchestra.

William Lloyd Webber's *Divine Compassion* (1945) was another work written in a traditional idiom at a time of sudden development of the language with the emergence of such brilliant scores as *A Child of Our Time* and, a little later, Benjamin Britten's *A Spring Symphony*. As is recounted on pages 66-70 Lloyd Webber responded by putting his music in a bottom drawer. Now, over 50 years on, and fuelled by the interest of his sons Andrew and Julian Lloyd Webber, his music is being heard again, and this substantial score could well prove a find for choral societies seeking a modern alternative for *The Crucifixion*.

During the competition several of the 'standards' of the British choral repertoire were also heard, music of place, possibly Gerald Finzi's *Intimations of Immortality* being the most atmospheric and sung in Hereford Cathedral where it was first heard in 1950. It was also particularly interesting to have Finzi's timeless Wordsworth setting sung in the same series that included Richard Rodney Bennett's 2001 setting, a treatment made, according to the composer, in a pre-concert discussion, in complete ignorance of Finzi.

Vaughan Williams's choral music is well-known, extensively recorded and widely sung. But several big works are heard much less frequently, perhaps the rarest being the excellent concert version of key numbers from his *The Pilgrim's Progress* which after the composer's death Christopher Morris and Roy Douglas assembled as *Pilgrim's Journey*. At a time when Vaughan Williams's 'morality' has been enjoying a new celebrity with Richard Hickox's excellent recording, this proved a worthwhile discovery of some familiar music albeit in unfamiliar juxtaposition. This is clearly a rewarding way for local choral societies to experience the powerful and varied music from the theatre in a concert performance.

The only work to be offered by more than one competitor was Sir George Dyson's *Agincourt*, a swaggering choral setting of very familiar words from Shakespeare's *Henry V*. This was doubtless thought a throwback when first heard in 1956, but it was very well played and sung on both occasions during the competition In the fairly compact space of St Mary Magdalene Church, Woodstock, where Paul Ingram and the Woodstock Music Society gave it great impact, it was also thrilling in the vast acoustic of Guildford Cathedral; it impressed all who heard it, for its varied choral writing, its memorable invention and its headlong pacing. Again a fairly short work, but one to be relished by choral societies everywhere.

The stylistic dividing line between the old and the new surely came in 1960, the year in which Benjamin Britten's *Cantata Academica* was first heard. Here we had a different kind of occasional music to that essayed by Dyson, and soon to be reinforced by the reception accorded Britten's *War Requiem* when performed in Coventry Cathedral in 1962.

Apart from Britten much of the new choral music from the mid-century has, for the moment, tended to be forgotten, and was less represented by the performances being discussed. Such big statements as David Blake's *Lumina* from 1959 and Paul Patterson's punchy 'Three Choirs Trilogy' – *Mass of the Sea, Stabat Mater* and *Te Deum* from the 1980s will surely have their day again. But one British composer who strides the choral landscape after 1960 was heard twice during the competition, and clearly deserves to be heard much more frequently. This was John Joubert, composer of the popular Christmas carol *Torches*, whose extended choral works were heard at the Three Choirs and elsewhere in the 1960s and 1970s. He enjoyed significant successes in the 1990s with his *Rochester Triptych* and *For the Beauty of the Earth*.

Three of his extended choral works Joubert designates as 'choral symphonies', and two of these were heard during the competition, both of them in prize-winning programmes. The performers' success with this repertoire reminded us of a significant body of worthwhile choral music which choirs everywhere would find it rewarding to explore. Perhaps the tougher nut to crack came with Joubert's 1968 Three Choirs' commission *The Choir Invisible*, the first of his choral symphonies. Joubert provides a marked contrast to Stanford's setting of the familiar words from Ecclesiastes, 'Let us now praise famous men', in *Ave Atque Vale*. Perhaps more immediately approachable was the third of the choral symphonies, his 1989 setting for Birmingham, *For the Beauty of the Earth*. Here Joubert writes a work of bounding intoxicating energy, which the Birmingham Festival Choral Society were singing for the third time, surely making it self-recommending for other choirs.

Among living choral composers Allan Bullard's minute-and-a-half unaccompanied *Cantata Gloria* of 1999, in popular style, provided an opener to put everyone in a good mood before the Woodstock Choral Society's excellent concerts. Perhaps the most familiar name was John Rutter, whose *Psalmfest* of 1993 consists of nine varied movements most of which had had an independent life in the previous decade or two. When heard as a coherent work (in fact the Stanmore Choral Society did seven of the nine movements) it made an impressive and substantial score, greater than the sum of its parts, which the choir clearly relished.

Richard Blackford's 5-minute 'Canticle of the Birds', the fifth movement of his St Francis of Assisi cantata, *Mirror of Perfection*, was a gorgeous 'lollipop' for tenor solo with chorus at Bury St Edmunds, reminding us that, as with *Psalmfest*, recent works need not be heard complete, and can yield delightful music of interest to performers and audience alike. Blackford, who some readers may remember as the composer of the engaging children's pageant-opera *Sir Gawain and the Green Knight*, recorded by Argo in 1979, had the advantage of having this score broadcast on BBC Television as well as being available on commercial CD, a recording strongly commended to programme planners.

Christopher Brown first became widely-known in the late 1970s with many new works, several heard on BBC Radio 3. But although he has continued writing it would be possible for choral society directors not to be aware of the range of his splendid catalogue of approachable choral works all very much choral society repertoire. This includes *Chauntecleer*, *Fair & Feast*, his unaccompanied Christmas sequence *Hodie Salvator Apparuit*, *Seascape* and *The Vision of Saul*. The 23-minute choral suite *The Circling Year*, heard at the Leith Hill Festival in 1999 is a typical example; its welling climax at the words 'and universal peace/Lie like a shaft of light across the land' proclaims a composer with an immediate appeal. At Cambridge we heard Brown's 'reflections at a new Millennium', *Invocation, Op 90* a recent choral setting for double choir with organ accompaniment 'celebrating the birth of Christ two thousand years ago'. Notable for a wide-ranging libretto which integrates words by Traherne, Gerald Manley Hopkins, Alice Meynell, Edith Sitwell, D H Lawrence and others into a continuous text is would make the perfect companion to Britten's *Rejoice in the Lamb*, by which it was followed at Cambridge.

Also written to reach a wide audience, Sir Richard Rodney Bennett's newly commissioned *The Glory and the Dream* set the same Wordsworth words as Finzi in his now classic *Intimations of Immortality*. In a pre-concert talk Richard Rodney Bennett admitted he had never heard the Finzi, and so approached his text without preconceptions. The composer told us that his conception of the piece preceded his discovery of Wordsworth's text. He said he was looking to evoke the transcendental quality of English countryside when viewed with a childlike innocence. 'Something very tonal, very clear, very bright – and I had the image of the morning of the world', so it is not surprising that when he found Wordsworth's poem in a verse anthology he thought 'that's the poem'. The 'opening images [of the poem] are so magical'.

The Millennium Choral Competition was conceived to explore worthwhile but forgotten music from the earlier decades of the twentieth century back into the nineteenth. It was a pleasurable surprise to be reminded by competitors of the vitality of the choral music scene today. The beginning of a new century has seen a resurgence of choral composition deserving exploration by performers everywhere. As Sir Arthur Bliss once observed 'talking about *new* music is about as sensible as talking about a new horse, we are surely interested in hearing the music of today'. I hope this exploration of repertoire written over more than a century and a quarter has demonstrated what a wonderfully rich heritage we have; it is not necessary constantly to sing the same restricted repertoire of old favourites, important though they are. In this handbook you will find programme notes and performance details of some thirty worthwhile works, they are but the tip of an iceberg. Happy hunting, and happy singing!

4. OBTAINING THE MUSIC
practical lessons from the competition

LEWIS FOREMAN

MANY OF THE CHOIRS PARTICIPATING IN THE MILLENNIUM CHORAL Competition experienced serious practical problems in obtaining the music for their concerts. These were all overcome and if you would like to explore any of the music whose performances are documented in these pages, please see pp 101-5 for details of where the necessary materials were found, and may now be obtained. Some years ago the British Music Society actually ran a seminar on this problem, and readers are referred to the published transcript for an interesting discussion of specific categories of material, and specific publishers (*Lost and Only Sometimes Found: a seminar on music publishing and archives*. BMS, 1992).

Problems are largely caused by the tremendous changes that have taken place in music publishing over the last twenty or thirty years, notably in the ownership and physical location of firms. This has resulted in material being withdrawn for a variety of reasons and, worse, long-established staff in hire libraries and promotion departments have been succeeded by newcomers, often without the practical experience of their forebears, usually totally dependent on fallible computer systems, and, apparently without any concern or first-hand passion about the music (or in one or two cases one might add, their employers)! Doubtless one day music publishers will wake up to the money they are losing because of this problem, but for the moment it is not helpful to be told by the hire library of this or that well-known publisher that a work is not theirs when the enquirer is actually holding a vocal score from a public library or second-hand shop bearing that publisher's imprint, or has found the piece in an advertisement from days gone by on the back cover of another work.

Perhaps the first decision which has to be made before setting out on planning a revival is to decide if the music to be performed is in copyright, as dealing with music out of copyright means that one can act without the necessity of seeking copyright permission and being constrained by the requirements of publisher or other interested parties. Copyright used to subsist for 50 years in the UK, but in the 1990s it was increased to 70 years. This means, for example, that Stanford (died 1924) and Parry (died 1918) are *out* of copyright, but

Elgar, Delius and Holst (who all died 1934), although for much of the 1980s were out of copyright, are at the time of writing again *in* copyright, which will finally expire at the end of 2004.

The various practical musical activities necessary for the mounting of such a choral performance fall into three categories:

· finding a source for multiple copies of the vocal scores;
· obtaining the full score;
· hiring the orchestral parts for the performance.

The majority of the music choral societies wish to perform will have been published at sometime, but in deciding how to source it for a performance there are many options which might well reduce the cost. The most effective of these is borrowing the set of vocal scores through one's local public library. Not all public libraries maintain collections of choral sets for loan, but there are a number of centres which have the force of national or regional collections and these are, in theory, available country-wide. Consulting the music librarian at your local public library (if your library still has one!) has to be one of the first actions in putting on a performance. Several participants in the competition obtained their vocal scores this way, though there was one disgraceful episode where a county library refused to loan the vocal scores to a choir in a neighbouring county, resulting in quite unnecessary expense for the choir concerned.

When you telephone the publisher of the vocal score about which you have been waxing increasingly enthusiastic at the piano and are told 'it's not ours', what do you do? While still speaking to the publisher it is a good idea to try to establish whether they have a record of it:

· do they still hold the rights (you may have to ask for the copyright department) and if not when were they relinquished;
· if they have an archive is there an archive copy of the score;
· talk to the promotions manager and see if they can be persuaded to investigate for you;
· try to establish contact with the composer's estate or family.

Choral works were often only published in vocal score, with the manuscript full score and orchestral parts being available on hire.

Even recently one has experienced some publishers still sending out composers' autograph manuscripts as the hire copy. Thus it only needed the one or two copies of these to be lost for the work to become unplayable in its original orchestration.

But many full scores of choral works did appear in print and often string parts were printed, as before, say 1930, printing was the most economical way of duplicating them. If any of these were printed then a copy will almost certainly have been deposited in the National Library - in the UK the British Library, in the USA the Library of Congress - and the catalogues of those institutions should be consulted when searching for an elusive item. At the very least this will give one some hard evidence when talking to the former publisher; it will also mean that a search in other libraries - the BBC, the conservatoires (particularly the Royal College of Music), university and major public libraries all being worth approaching. It is also worth trying the libraries of the major orchestras, the most likely to hold the sort of repertoire described in this book being the Bournemouth Symphony Orchestra.

The Scottish Music Archive in Glasgow enabled one competitor to programme a chosen work by supplying the full score and orchestral of W G Whittaker's *The Cælestial Spheare*, once available from Oxford University Press. Unfortunately the Welsh Music Centre is no longer active as a practical source for obtaining performing materials while the British Music Information Centre in London, which is very active, tends to deal with late twentieth century works rather than those from an earlier period, but is still a useful source of expertise and a referral centre for material it does not cover.

When undertaking a significant revival, it is usually worthwhile approaching the estate or surviving family, or the author of a major book on the composer (inevitably an enthusiast with wide-ranging contacts). It should also not be forgotten to establish whether there is a charitable trust promoting the composer concerned. As well as the usual NFMS, Lottery, regional and local authority funding and corporate support from local firms, several societies in the competition successfully sought help with both music and funding from, among others, the trusts representing the estates of Bainton, Delius, Vaughan Williams, Dyson and Frank Bridge. While these all provided funding, some also helped with tracing and obtaining performing materials.

When presenting music by a living composer it is often the case that the performing materials are available from the composer personally, or from a small imprint dealing with a few names or just one composer, as in the case of Christopher Brown who is published by Musography.

In one case the full score and parts were no longer available from the publisher. This was Frédéric d'Erlanger's *Messe de Requiem* formerly published by Schott. Enquiries to Schott established that although d'Erlanger is still in copyright and that the vocal score had been published by them in 1930, they had returned the work to the composer's estate and only held a few copies of the first and second violin parts. Their copyright department could not even give a current address for the composer's family and estate. However contact was eventually made with the family who provided a photocopy of the full score but had no orchestral parts. However, they gave permission to programme it and Schott's provided the violin parts they held and a few vocal scores. In this case new parts were written out by hand and by using Sibelius software and the choir printed a supply of vocal scores from the few copies that had been traced: such is the enthusiasm to overcome all obstacles! Here the parts were written at no cost (other than photocopying) to the performance by a volunteer, though if the funding had been available employing a professional copyist would have been an option.

In one or two cases material now out of copyright was privately held, and while readily provided for performance the owners preferred that any approaches for future performances should be made via the British Music Society. These are so identified in the list on pp 101-5. The BMS will be pleased to route enquiries from future intending performers.

5. PROGRAMME NOTES
for the works performed

THE PROGRAMME NOTES FOR THE CHORAL WORKS PERFORMED during the competition are here reprinted as a guide to performing groups wishing to explore this and similar repertoire. The notes are reprinted unchanged from the various choirs' printed programmes, other than for correcting occasional literals and deleting obvious duplication between similar notes for different works by the same composer. The notes have been arranged in chronological order of composition.

The notes are by the following and are signed by initials. We are grateful to the various authors for permission to use their contributions here:

Christopher Brown (CB)
Lewis Foreman (LF)
John Gibbons (JG)
Anthony R Gibbs (ARG)
Tony Giles (TG)
David Gould (DG)
Garry Humphreys (GPH)
David Lyle (DL)
Diana McVeagh (DMV)
Harrison Oxley (HO)
Jeremy Patterson (JP)

MILLENNIUM CHORAL COMPETITION

List of works heard in chronological order of composition

Sullivan: *Te Deum Laudamus* (1872)
Sullivan: *The Golden Legend* (1885)
Parry: *Blest Pair of Sirens* (1887)
Bainton: *Before Sunrise* (1906/19)
Vaughan Williams: *Toward the Unknown Region* (1907)
Delius: *Songs of Sunset* (1909)
Stanford: *Ave Atque Vale* (1909)
Parry: *Ode on the Nativity* (1912)
Elgar: *The Music Makers* (1912)
Dale: *Before the Paling of the Stars* (1912)
Parry: *The Chivalry of the Sea* (1916)
Bridge: *A Prayer* (1916-18)
W G Whittaker: *Célestial Spheare* (1923)
d'Erlanger: *Requiem* (1930)
Oldroyd: *Jhesu Christ, St Mary's Sone* (1931)
Britten: *Rejoice in the Lamb* (1943)
Berkeley: *Festival Anthem* (1945)
Finzi: *Lo the Full Final Sacrifice* (1945)
Le Fleming: *Five Psalms* (1945)
Lloyd Webber: *Divine Compassion* (1945)
Finzi: *Intimations of Immortality* (1950)
Vaughan Williams: *Pilgrim's Journey* (1950 rev 1964)
Rubbra: *Song of the Soul* (1952)
Dyson: *Agincourt* (1956)
Britten: *Cantata Academica* (1960)
Joubert: *The Choir Invisible* (1968)
Joubert: *For the Beauty of the Earth* (1985)
John Rutter: *Psalmfest (*1993)
Christopher Brown: *Invocation* (1999)
Alan Bullard: *Cantate Gloria* (1999)
Blackford: *Canticle of the Birds* (1999)
Richard Rodney Bennett: *The Glory and the Dream* (2001)

SIR ARTHUR SULLIVAN (1842-1900)
TE DEUM LAUDAMUS
[*FESTIVAL TE DEUM*]
for soprano, chorus & orchestra

1. *We Praise Thee, O God* (chorus)
2. *To Thee Cherubim* (soprano solo & chorus)
3. *The Glorious Company of the Apostles* (chorus)
4. *When Thou Tookest Upon Thee* (soprano solo)
5. *We Believe That Thou Shalt Come* (soprano solo & chorus)
6. *O Lord, Save Thy People* (chorus)
7. *Vouchsafe, O Lord* (chorus)

WE GENERALLY REMEMBER SULLIVAN FOR HIS COLLABORATION with W S Gilbert. They met in 1869 and first collaborated in 1871, producing the Savoy Operas, a relationship recently brought vividly to life in the film *Topsy Turvy*. However, Sullivan wrote an extensive catalogue of music with serious intentions: oratorios, orchestral music, a symphony, songs, hymn tunes, and the opera *Ivanhoe*, and he was one of the most successful British composers of his day.

From a musical family, Sullivan was a member of the Chapel Royal Choir at 12, published an anthem at 13 and won the Mendelssohn Scholarship at the Royal Academy of Music a year later. Aspiring, like all British music students of his day, to study in Germany, he attended the Leipzig Conservatoire and at the age of 20 became the organist of St Michael's, Chester Square, and was celebrated for his incidental music for *The Tempest*, a sensation for the young composer in 1861.

The work we hear tonight was Sullivan's first setting of the *Te Deum*; later came a liturgical setting for the Chester festival in 1897, and in 1900, the year of his death, he produced a *Te Deum* as a thanksgiving for victory in the Boer War. The memory of Albert, the Prince Consort, who died of typhoid in December 1861, must have been strong when ten years later his son the Prince of Wales (later King Edward VII) fell seriously ill with the same disease, and his recovery was marked with a Day of Thanksgiving and various state celebrations. Sullivan composed this *Te Deum* for the Festival concert held at the Crystal Palace on 1 May 1872, when 2,000 performers presented it in the main transept before an audience of

26,000. One can imagine that so clear cut a score, in so popular a style, performed by so large a choir and orchestra, with a military band and the mighty Crystal Palace organ, must have created an overwhelming impression.

Sullivan, by virtue of his musical prowess, had been a personal friend of the Prince of Wales for a number of years – and through the good offices of another aristocratic musical intimate, the Duke of Edinburgh, he was allowed to dedicate the work to Queen Victoria – Sullivan always had an eye not only to the emotional temperature of the time, but also to the business opportunities of his various contacts.

In this work Sullivan wrote in his most extrovert and popular style, and the music constantly hints that he would have preferred to be writing for the stage. Certainly he did not produce a solemn religious work for a solemn state occasion, he even managed largely to avoid the religioso overtones which colour his oratorios and cantatas. What we have is a hugely enjoyable, at places quasi-operatic, celebration.

The marching opening, with organ (which will return to introduce the last movement) leads quickly into a choral setting which alternates the block harmonies of a hymn (Sullivan wrote many favourite hymns) with a contrapuntal fugal texture which on its second appearance is worked into an ambitious climactic setting of 'To thee all Angels cry aloud'. In the following soprano solo, 'To Thee Cherubim', the characteristic triplets in the solo line give it an impetus which carries the music forward with the hint of a lighter style, while the solemn block harmonies of the chorus create a suitably contrasted atmosphere.

The following fast chorus 'The glorious company of the apostles' incorporates a Gregorian plainsong tune, used in a quite Victorian and Sullivanesque way, and driven along by a typical accompanying orchestral texture. Sullivan follows that exhilarating movement with another catchy number, and the earlier suspicion of a lighter agenda is reinforced, when in the soprano solo 'When thou tookest upon', Sullivan sets over an oompha accompaniment on the strings, a catchy popular-style tune with 'operatic' rising semitones and an accompanying counter melody, which could indeed be from a stage work. Why indeed, should the devil have all the best tunes?

These hints of Sullivan's subsequent development can also be heard in the chorus 'We believe', where the after the solemn opening block harmonies the 6/8 accompaniment in lilting quavers again seems to be leading us into the accompaniment of an operetta song. Sullivan succeeds in this work by the vigour and energy of his setting, and the penultimate movement opens with the soprano's soft prayer for salvation and blessing, answered by the choir in conventional block harmonies, but is soon contrasted with the catchy vigour of the quick fugal setting of 'Day by day' which sweeps all along with irresistible momentum, the 'Day by day' theme transferring to the orchestra when the chorus have a more solemn setting.

In his final movement Sullivan uses the hymn tune *St Anne* ('O God our help in ages past'). At first it is presented 'straight' and after another fast fugal passage to which *St Anne* becomes a counterpoint on trumpet, the composer introduces a popular instrumental interlude scored for ad lib military band, a quick march, almost a quadrille. The juxtaposition of these, the march accompanying *St Anne* in popular style, strongly suggests an operetta finale. One can imagine that in the Crystal Palace, with huge numbers of performers and a large military band, the effect must have been intoxicating; no wonder it was a great success, and it is difficult to understand why it is unknown today and has never had a professional recording.

LF

Sir Arthur Sullivan (1842-1900)
THE GOLDEN LEGEND
for soprano (Elsie), alto (Ursula), tenor (Prince Henry) and baritone (Lucifer/Forester), chorus & orchestra

In 1866, the twenty-four year old Arthur Sullivan had accepted an invitation to write an orchestral work for the Norwich Festival, which appears to have filled him with rather less than enthusiasm and for which he felt little inspiration. In August, he wrote to his father, Thomas, for whom he had the deepest affection and whom he regarded as his best friend, that the idea of writing an abstract work 'in cold blood ...with nothing suggestive to work upon' was not at all to his liking and that he felt he should abandon the commission. With the understanding and kindness characteristic of him, his father replied immediately, spurring his son to continued effort and suggesting that something would probably occur which would 'put new vigour and fresh thoughts into him. Tragically, that 'something' did occur, when, a few days later, Thomas Sullivan died of an aneurysm, plunging the composer into

Sullivan: the closing bars of the third part of *The Golden Legend*, the chorus enter at the end of Elsie's aria 'The night is calm and cloudless'.

deep and inconsolable grief.

Twenty years later, on 16 October, 1886, the now Sir Arthur Sullivan (firmly established as England's leading composer, and with the success of *The Mikado*, first heard in 1885, still ringing in his ears) took the platform to conduct the first performance of *The Golden Legend*, in Leeds. He had been conductor of the Leeds Musical Festival since 1880 and, as a composer, had scored a considerable success there, in that year, with his sacred musical drama, *The Martyr of Antioch*, whose libretto had been arranged, from Henry Hart Milman's poem, by W S Gilbert.

The commission which was to lead to *The Golden Legend* was first mooted in 1884, when he was asked – as he had been for Norwich, in 1866 – for an orchestral piece. Once again, however, the writing of purely instrumental music proved much less congenial to Sullivan's creative temperament than the setting of words to music, and he asked the festival committee if he could write a choral work instead.

Having obtained their approval, Sullivan cast around for a suitable subject, and was eventually led to Henry Wadsworth Longfellow's narrative poem, *The Golden Legend*, by a close personal and business friend, Miss Chappell (who was, we presume, the daughter of Tom Chappell, the music publisher).

Characteristically, Sullivan put off making a final decision on his choice of subject (no doubt causing sleepless nights for the committee) until only nine months remained before the Festival date, when, at last, he sought the help of the journalist and *Daily Telegraph* music critic, Joseph Bennett, and asked him to examine the poem with a view to producing a 'book' from the poem. This Bennett did, and Sullivan finally began composition in April, somehow managing to fit the necessary hours at his desk into a work schedule which was punishing by any standards, and completing the work on August 25.

The first performance was rapturously received, by public and critics alike, and the work soared to phenomenal heights of popularity, being performed seventeen times in Britain, in the twelve months following its premiere, and admired by Elgar and Stanford. By the end of the 19th century, it had been heard more than three hundred times, in Britain, the United States, South Africa, Australia, New Zealand, Germany, the Netherlands and Sweden and, in the century's last decade, overtook Mendelssohn's *Elijah* for second place (to Handel's *Messiah*) in popularity with choral societies and the general public.

As with *In Memoriam*, however, the rapidly changing tastes of the 20th century, and a somewhat neurotic reaction against the whole Victorian ethos have caused *The Golden Legend* to disappear from the concert platform and tonight's performance will be – to the best of my knowledge – the first, in Scotland, for at least fifty years. Bennett's libretto divides the story of *The Golden Legend* (taken from the mythological tale by the 12th century Minnesinger, Hartmann von der Aue) into six scenes, plus a Prologue and Epilogue, each of which is through-composed and comes to a full-close, with no musical links between the scenes. Sullivan manages, however, to provide structural unity by employing two formal devices – one, a system of cross-scene themes, in the manner of Wagnerian 'leitmotiven', which serve as musical 'reminders' of the characters to which they refer, and the other, a scheme of tonality to bind the separate scenes.

Bennett's vastly reduced text undoubtedly limited the musical possibilities available to Sullivan, and, more seriously, undermined the story's dramatic credibility – Elsie's decision to offer her life for that of the Prince, for example, appears a sudden whim on her part, and his response as less than grateful, to say the least, a situation not found in Longfellow's original, where the characters are much more deeply drawn. Inevitably, this caused problems for Sullivan, who was unable to do much with the characters and provided music which, though generally apt, created somewhat two-dimensional and anonymous portraits. Where he excels, vocally, however, is when he has the opportunity to put his innate lyrical gifts to work, to create vivid, engaging and beautiful miniature tone-pictures, which completely and effortlessly capture the mood of the moment.

Sullivan obviously revelled in the orchestral opportunities afforded by the cantata and its subject matter, and it is undoubtedly his treatment of the orchestra which is the work's crowning glory. It is masterly throughout and reveals remarkable levels of inspiration and subtlety, with the string parts, in particular, characterised by passages of complex figurations quite without precedent in any of his previous scores.

Though the influence of the Savoy operas is evident throughout – including, for example, the famous 'double-chorus' technique (used in Scene III, between Lucifer and a chorus of pilgrims) – it is worth noting that the operas which followed *The Golden Legend* were, in turn, affected by the significant development of technique which Sullivan experienced as a result of writing the cantata. The 'Ghost' music, in *Ruddigore*, for example (criticised by Gilbert for being too serious), with its descriptive orchestral effects, surely flows from the stormy Prologue and its depiction of Lucifer's increasingly desperate attempts to demolish the cathedral. Indeed, the whole of the 'Ghost' scene displays a harmonic palette and orchestral adventurousness which Sullivan could hardly have been expected to attain, without the experience of the cantata's composition behind him.

The chorus – in a work written as a festive cantata – is surprisingly limited in its appearance, but its contributions are always telling and provide some of the most memorable passages in the score, including the concluding section of Scene III and, of course, the main unison theme and fugue, in the Epilogue, whose sweep and exuberant confidence are at one with those of the final bars of *In Memoriam*.

DLL

Sir Hubert Parry (1848-1918)
BLEST PAIR OF SIRENS
for chorus & orchestra

Parry and Stanford are often linked as pillars of the establishment, for Parry was Professor at Oxford and Director of the Royal College of Music, and an even more prolific composer than Stanford. His great melody *Jerusalem* and the incomparable coronation anthem *I was glad,* seem set to assure him of a place among the immortals of British music.

As conductor of the [London] Bach Choir, Stanford persuaded the committee to commission a short work from Parry for a concert in 1887, and it was George Grove [of dictionary fame] who suggested this Milton ode. As well as showing high technical mastery in writing for 8-part voices, Parry reveals a profound insight into the structure and inspiration of the words. Milton's verse and Parry's voice are indeed a blest pair, lifting us radiantly to celestial joy.

HO

RALPH VAUGHAN WILLIAMS (1872-1858)
TOWARD THE UNKNOWN REGION
for chorus & orchestra

Bach was behind the times, Beethoven was ahead of them, and yet both were the greatest of composers. Modernism and conservatism are irrelevant. What matters is to be true to oneself.
                                Vaughan Williams to the Composers' Guild, 1957

Vaughan Williams is one of the most important British composers of the twentieth century. Well-known for such immortal masterpieces as *The Lark Ascending, Fantasia on a Theme of Thomas Tallis* as well as great hymns: *For all the Saints,* he has for too long been tagged by many in the musical world with the label English 'cowpat' school. Anyone who knows the nine symphonies, in particular the Fourth, Sixth and Ninth, would know that the cows of England must have been in serious trouble long ago for such a generalisation to apply to a whole musical style. Vaughan Williams stamped his personality on all that he undertook and, in so doing, communicated to both the unsophisticated and the professionals of his art. Both Holst and he led the way for English music to free itself from the domination of German music and to allow composers to find their own language of expression.

As the distinguished writer Michael Kennedy has written: 'In many respects his music is best viewed as a reconciliation of opposites: of restlessness and tranquillity, of brusque, direct expression and serene, visionary meditation, of anger and humour'.

Toward the Unknown Region was the first work of Vaughan Williams to establish him as a force to be reckoned with. It is a setting of a poem by the American poet Walt Whitman whose work found such favour with British composers of the time (*Sea Drift* by Delius and *A Sea Symphony* by Vaughan Williams are perhaps the two most well-known settings). In 1905 both Holst and Vaughan Williams began setting this episode from *Whispers of Heavenly Death*. On completion in 1906 they both decided that Vaughan Williams's setting was the best and he subsequently submitted it to the Leeds Festival where he conducted its premiere on the 10 October 1907 to great acclaim.

JG

Frederick Delius (1862-1934)
SONGS OF SUNSET
for baritone, mezzo-soprano, chorus & orchestra

The 'Englishness' of English music is a strangely subjective matter, particularly in the case of Delius. His parents were Dutch and German and, although he was born in Bradford, he made all efforts to escape as soon as possible and spent the rest of his life abroad, in Florida, Leipzig, Paris and, ultimately, at Grez-sur-Loing near Fontainebleau. His music reflects his life in these exotic places, susceptible as he was to the beauties of nature, and to the emotions, joys and sorrows of life. Furthermore, 'form' (of the sort that would have been instilled in him had he joined his contemporaries in studying with Parry and Stanford at the Royal College of Music) has no place in his music, in which he seeks sensuous beauty of sound from moment to moment. It took an interpreter of the calibre of Sir Thomas Beecham to convince contemporary audiences of the innate and highly individual dramatic nature of these pieces. As one of Beecham's distinguished successors, Vernon Handley, has put it, contrary to popular assumptions Delius is not floppy!

Songs of Sunset has been described by Delius's friend, biographer and fellow composer Philip Heseltine ('Peter Warlock') as 'a lover's requiem over lost illusions', and the theme – the transience of human life and love, and the 'longing for the perpetuation of impossible bliss' (Fenby) – is one that inspired many of Delius's greatest works (*Appalachia, Koanga,* and *Sea Drift* in particular). We have to thank Jelka Delius for this piece, for it was one that resulted from her custom of leaving on his desk texts she had selected in the hope of inspiring his muse. Ernest Dowson, whose melancholy poems of love were very popular for a time, like Delius was more at home in France than in England and so in many respects had much in common with the composer, who set several of his poems.

The first chorus focuses on three images of ending: a winter's day, the setting sun and a faded flower. The baritone soloist addresses his love in a tone of rapturous melancholy, wishing to prolong one moment for ever, or even to die, rather than undergo the inevitable decay of time. The chorus 'Pale amber sunlight' then creates the image of an autumn day in which the lover seems to welcome the 'twilight of the heart', as if resigned to the inevitable approach of death. In the following soprano solo we hear the sorrow of an imminent parting, while the baritone laments the loss of love beside 'the waters of separation'. Then the chorus sings of the renewal of spring while the two solo voices grieve for the departure of love. The baritone soloist then revisits a past love in memory, finds it becoming fainter and more distant, yet cannot quite forget. Finally Dowson's most famous poem speaks of the brief and fleeting nature of human life, itself emerging from and closing in 'a dream'.*

The music provides an example of how Delius could achieve a feeling of unity and cohesion m his works without imposing a formal structure. Apart from one 'forlorn little theme' (first heard on flute and cor anglais at 'Faded it *lies* in the dust') which recurs throughout, there are no other thematic links. Furthermore, Delius saw the chorus and orchestra as related members of one body of musical sound and tried (unsuccessfully) to have the chorus seated while singing, 'to lend colour to the illusion of impersonal unity'.

Songs of Sunset (originally called *Songs of Twilight)* was one of Beecham's favourite works and was first performed by him at a Delius concert in Queen's Hall, London, in 1911.

* *I am grateful to Christine Webb for the use in this paragraph of her synopsis of the poems which she prepared for members of the choir.*

GPH

EDGAR BAINTON (1880-1956)
BEFORE SUNRISE
symphony for contralto solo, chorus and orchestra

EDGAR BAINTON WAS BORN IN LONDON AND WON A SCHOLARSHIP to the Royal College of Music where he studied with Stanford, Walford Davies, Charles Wood and Franklin Taylor. In 1901 (age 21) he became Professor for Pianoforte and Composition at the Newcastle upon Tyne Conservatory, where he remained (becoming Principal in 1912) until in 1934 he emigrated to Australia to take up the post of Director of the Sydney State Conservatory. In the meantime, he conducted the Newcastle Philharmonic Orchestra from 1912 and was among the many British musicians stranded on the Continent at the outbreak of the First World War in 1914 who were interned at

Ruhleben Camp in Germany until the end of hostilities four years later.

Bainton began work on *Before Sunrise in* 1907, a month after his choral work *The Blessed Damozel*, and completed it on 6 December. For some reason unexplained by the composer (unless, as Lewis Foreman has suggested, he felt it to be overshadowed by Vaughan Williams's *A Sea Symphony,* produced in 1910), it lay unperformed until, during the War, the Carnegie United Kingdom Trust announced a scheme for publishing large-scale music by British composers and Bainton, incarcerated in Ruhleben, decided to revive it as an entry for the first competition in 1917, where it won one of the six awards. Subsequently, Stainer & Bell published the vocal score in 1921 and the full score in 1922. The first performance was given in Newcastle Town Hall on 6 April 1921 by the Newcastle and Gateshead Choral Society ('Chorus of 250 Voices'!) conducted by the composer. It was an occasion considered by the correspondent of *The Times* to be 'worth a special journey to Newcastle to hear' and he reported that 'the production was received with every sign of enthusiasm by the audiences', no doubt rooting for the local man.

Bainton admitted in his own programme note that 'the theme is one that makes a strong appeal to the composer: the freeing of humanity from enslavement, the bettering of conditions of life, and visions of a more idealistic destiny than at present [1921] seems likely or possible'. After his wartime experiences one assumes that this was something about which he would have felt even more strongly in 1921 than in 1907.

The first movement is purely orchestral, and in it are laid out the various themes and ideas that pervade the entire work. Bainton has described how it begins with chaos, from which grows Life and Death; the transfiguration of Death through Love and the victory of the Soul of Man; the coming of humanity, culminating in the coming of Christ; the woes under which the vast majority of humanity suffers; then faith in the ultimate freedom of mankind and in the realisation of its possibilities of happiness and spirituality. Thematically, the heaving night is suggested by the heavy, slow-moving passage with which the work opens; then follows a premonition of the Death theme; a more agitated passage is associated with the idea of the creation of Life; and after 'a loud and troublous treatment' of the heaving waters theme, the full orchestra bursts forth with the Life theme in its full form.

Bainton's note continues: 'A quieter section speaks of the "Joy of

Life", later a cor anglais solo of the "Sorrows of Life", and afterwards a long sustained horn solo is intended to speak of "Love, the Crown of Life". The dream *is* shattered by a struggle between life and death, in which most of the themes already heard are developed. After a climax is reached the music quickly dies down to a pianissimo, out of which a new theme issues on the cellos, "Death, transfigured by Love". This gives place to "Love, the Crown of Life". Ten closing fortissimo bars announce the theme of the "Victory of the Soul of Man".'

In the rest of the symphony the music is a reflection of the texts of Swinburne's poems (from his *Songs before Sunrise)*. The Victory theme most often is heard, thundered out in the second movement at the mention of Christ and at the line 'Liberty there is the light'; whispered when the question 'what of the night?' is asked of Liberty, in anticipation of the answer to come; and throughout the Finale (forte at the opening and in a choral and orchestral version at the end, reminiscent of the conclusion of the first movement).

The Man from *The Times* was clearly impressed, regarding this 'work of large scope and individual imagination' as 'in the nature of a great crescendo of feeling, from the first groping chords of the opening movement to [the] exuberant ending . . . The composer is not afraid of a direct and simple kind of expression when it suits his purpose, and . . . he convinces one of the genuineness of his feeling and his power of big achievement. It is a work which ought to be given by the larger choral societies of the country.'

GPH

SIR CHARLES VILLERS STANFORD (1852-1924)
AVE ATQUE VALE
for chorus & organ

STANFORD CAME FROM A CULTURED PROTESTANT FAMILY IN Dublin. Although a classicist, at Cambridge he came into his own as a musician, becoming organist of Trinity College at the age of 21, and Professor of Music in the University at 35. In the early 1870s he came like a gale of fresh air, with boundless enthusiasm and energy; extended visits to Germany gave him a wide circle of contacts with the leading musicians of the day.

Celebrated for 40 years as Professor of Composition at the Royal

College of Music, Stanford taught almost all the leading names of the following two generations. Apart from his fine settings for the cathedral service, his own works in all classical forms, including many operas, have been largely forgotten; however, today they are enjoying a considerable renaissance in radio and on record.

When the [London] Bach Choir commissioned Stanford to celebrate the centenary of the death of Haydn (1809), the composer took the opportunity also to mark the birth of Tennyson (in the same year), whose poetry he had set on various occasions, notably in the once widely popular cantata *The Revenge*. For this occasional memorial piece Stanford adopted the unusual title 'choral overture', and completed *Ave Atque Vale* (literally Hail and Farewell) in January 1909, setting Ecclesiasticus 43 and 44. In tribute, Stanford incorporates Haydn's Austrian hymn (popular in this country as the hymn tune 'Glorious things of Thee are spoken'). This is featured in the extended orchestral introduction, and fragments of it inform the thematic material throughout. The tune finally sings out in the orchestra at the end, to underline the words 'Their name liveth to all generations'.

LF

SIR C H H PARRY (1848-1918)
ODE ON THE NATIVITY
for soprano, chorus & orchestra

ON SEPTEMBER 12TH 1912, THE AUDIENCES AT THE HEREFORD Three Choirs Festival were treated to two premiere performances of English choral works, namely Vaughan Williams's *Fantasia on Christmas Carols* at the evening concert, and at the afternoon concert the delightful *Ode on the Nativity* by Hubert Parry, arguably one of his finest choral compositions which really deserves to be brought out of the shadow of *Blessed Pair of Sirens*, and be far better known. Incidentally Parry wrote that day in his diary: 'Vaughan Williams's piece very jolly'. History has not allowed us to know what RVW thought of his master's *Ode; doubtless* if an opinion was expressed it could not have been other than complimentary.

By the time that this very symphonic *Ode* was written, Parry had acquired considerable experience of writing in this genre. As with Handel, there is a bewildering variety of types to be found in Parry's

Stanford's *Ave Atque Vale*

choral compositions. He was constantly experimenting and constantly rethinking the problems of writing works for chorus and orchestra, and achievements laid the groundwork for Elgar, Vaughan Williams (his most illustrious pupil), Howells and Walton. They were also a sure preparation for this *Ode on the Nativity*. All of the consummate craft gathered from a lifetime of experience in composition is displayed in the work without any ostentation. By 1912, which also saw the premiere of his Fifth Symphony, he was only half a dozen years before his death; his creative output was at its height and had almost been completed. Still to come, however, were a highly individual setting of Psalm 46, *God is our Hope* (1913), a rather strange but stirring tone-poem in two movements *From Death to Life* (1914) and the glorious unaccompanied *Songs* of *Farewell* (1918).

The overall structure suggested by William Dunbar's poem 'Ode on the Nativity' is related most of all to the massive adagio spans of Bruckner and to the early tone-poems of Richard Strauss. It is worth noting that Parry could have chosen a Milton ode, but preferred Dunbar's because it offered greater rhythmic variety and, of course, a bigger challenge, in response to which he produced a highly contrapuntal and elaborate work. Each of Dunbar's six stanzas ends ' . . . *nobis Puer natus est*', which each time inspired Parry to a moment of dedicated intensity. The splendid dancing melodic ideas, similar to, but subtly different from each other, are moulded together with a sureness of touch which rivals the finest Elgar. The rich but delicate orchestration is influenced by Brahms and Mendelssohn, and to a lesser extent by Wagner and Liszt.

From the great climax which begins with the words 'Sing, heaven Imperial, most of height!' to the inwardly luminous coda with its solo bass clarinet, we can feel that Parry, in some ways a troubled agnostic, never forgot that innocence which leads a child to accept the star at the top of a Christmas tree as real.

ARG

Sir Edward Elgar (1857-1934)
THE MUSIC MAKERS, OP 69
for mezzo-soprano, chorus & orchestra

ELGAR COMPLETED THE VOCAL SCORE OF *THE MUSIC MAKERS*, HIS penultimate big choral work, on 18 July 1912, and orchestrated it during the following month for the first performance at the Birmingham Festival (to be the last such Festival for it was not re-established until long after the First World War) on 1 October that year. This reflected the pattern of the writing of Elgar's major choral works over the previous 15 years, which seems to have been established by their composition in fulfilment of commissions for major Edwardian choral festivals – most of them at Birmingham – which had the effect of giving Elgar comparatively short deadlines, which he had to meet. Inevitably in most cases this presented his publishers, Novello, with a headache in preparing printed vocal scores and performing materials in time. Elgar tended to push his delivery ever nearer the last possible moment, a problem that went some way towards causing the near disaster of the first performance of *The Dream of Gerontius* in 1900.

Elgar first assumed his characteristic voice with his orchestral overture *Froissart*, performed at Worcester in 1890, and we rather vaguely tend to remember that Elgar then quickly consolidated this reputation with a string of early choral works. However, while *The Black Knight* (dated 1892) first appeared at Worcester in April 1893, there was in fact a gap, and it was 1896 before this process of a regular succession of new choral works began in earnest.

In 1896 three new Elgar choral works appeared – *In the Bavarian Highlands* at Worcester in April, *Lux Christi* (*The Light of Life*) also at Worcester in September and *King Olaf* at Hanley at the end of October. Elgar was soon commissioned by the Leeds Festival, possibly the leading festival of the day, to write *Caractacus* which itself persuaded Birmingham to commission *The Dream of Gerontius* for the Birmingham Festival (which also thought of itself as the leader) at the beginning of October 1900. Elgar was back at Birmingham in 1903 with *The Apostles* and 1906 with *The Kingdom*, but was subsequently preoccupied with orchestral music, including most of his greatest works.

Thus it was an obvious initiative for Birmingham in 1912 to

Sir C H H Parry (1848-1918)
THE CHIVALRY OF THE SEA
a Naval Ode set to music for five part chorus and orchestra

Charles Hubert Hastings Parry, Eton and Oxford, despite his superficially patrician persona, was in fact a considerable radical, both politically and artistically. While early on he took a position with Lloyds Register of Shipping, he was no businessman and soon relinquished it for music. Director of the Royal College of Music after the death of its founder Sir George Grove, Parry was the key figure in the development of a characteristically English school of composition in the late nineteenth century. Parry is sometimes seen as an archetypal exponent of British-stiff-upper-lippishness in his music, but as this work shows, this was far from the case.

However, Parry found himself as a composer under the influence of Edward Dannreuther, a celebrated pianist of his day, whose influence in late nineteenth century musical Britain is only now becoming generally apparent. Parry was, as he freely admitted, very much a Teuton in his musical outlook, fluent in German and fully engaged with the example of German music, and an important pioneer of the revival and reassessment of earlier composers such as Bach and Schütz, looking to them as models.

For many years after his death, commentators only grudgingly admitted him to be an Important Historical Figure, when his music was little played apart from *Jerusalem*, *Blest Pair of Sirens* and *I Was Glad*, plus hymns, church music, organ pieces and a few songs. We were led to believe that his major choral music was beyond revival and the orchestral music merely footnotes in history books. Over the last twenty years this view has been slowly changed as the music has been played again, perhaps the climax coming with the revival and recording of the Piano Concerto which Dannreuther first played in 1880.

Parry wrote more than two dozen extended works for chorus and orchestra, and although himself agnostic, and self-confessedly not in sympathy with the British oratorio tradition, found himself the recipient of endless commissions for the leading choral festivals of the day. His first big commission, setting the revolutionary Shelley's *Prometheus Unbound*, had been seen in 1880 as a major turning point. He turned to the King James Bible for suitable stories and the language in which to clothe them. Delius's gibe 'Parry will set the whole Bible to music' was manifestly unfair, as it was Parry who really began the later practice, brought to perfection by his pupil Vaughan Williams, of anthologising English literature for musical setting.

The Chivalry of the Sea was written for the concert given on 12 December 1916 to remember those who had died at the Battle of Jutland, when the programme consisted of the Parry, Vaughan Williams's *A Sea Symphony* and Stanford's *Songs of the Fleet*, the latter with its affecting final 'Farewell'. The Poet Laureate, Robert Bridges' specially-written poem, dedicated to the memory of Charles Fisher, 'late student of Christ Church, Oxford' as the score tells us, an Oxford friend dead with a thousand others when the *Invincible* exploded at Jutland, still catches a certain brooding regret, though not without sentiments which do not find a ready acceptance today, such as 'And a great glory at heart that none can take away'.

The dark sea-swell of Parry's orchestral introduction creates the scene from the outset. Parry was a sailor, never happier than when on his yawl *The Wanderer*. Not for Parry the train and ferry to Ireland, he would sail there! So this is very much the voice of a man with first-hand knowledge of the sea, its constantly changing moods, its slow swell and undertow, relishing white water and never happier than when running before a following wind. This score packs these very varied moods into its fourteen-minute compass.

While the overall feeling is elegiac, the 'beefy' Parry is also in evidence, as at the words 'Ye man with armour'd patience'. Alongside comes typical scherzando writing, the vocal lines almost becoming sea shanties, and with the sense of a great hymn trying to emerge. There are several passages of vocal counterpoint in five parts (the sopranos are divided throughout), fugatos which, for an unfamiliar audience, make it difficult to follow the words; rather we perceive the outline, the sense of moving textures, the piquant harmonic colour. At the end Parry is almost beyond words, the return of the deep swelling opening theme, throat-catching in its sudden inflection, as with a sense of the infinite, we find Parry musing on lost friends, sailing ever on 'under starry skies', and the mourner turns suddenly away, unable to bear more.

LF

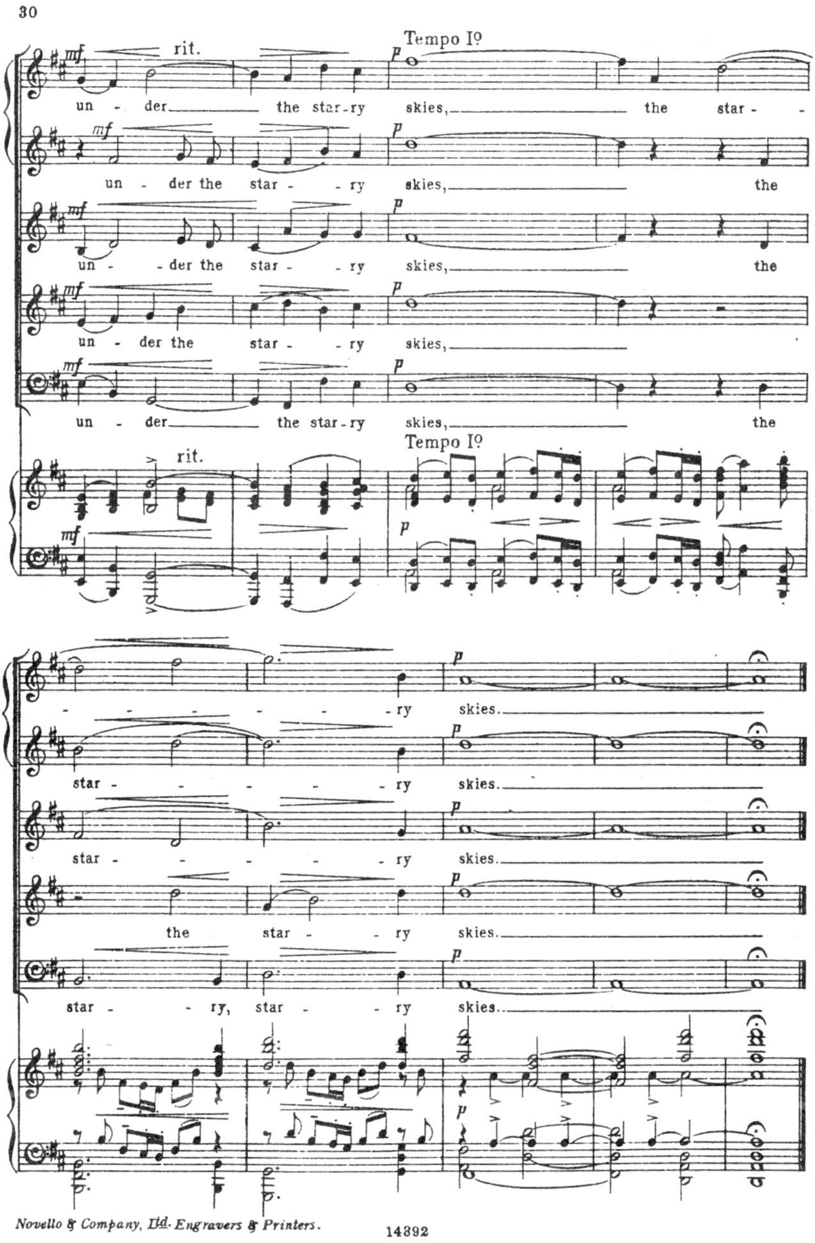

Parry's *The Chivalry of the Sea*: the evocative closing bars

FRANK BRIDGE (1879-1941)
A PRAYER
for chorus & orchestra

FRANK BRIDGE CAME FROM A MUSICAL FAMILY, THE TENTH OF twelve children. Bridge's father was a violin teacher and musical hall conductor in Brighton, and Frank was involved in practical music-making from an early age, playing in his father's orchestras and even conducting. Although he went to the Royal College of Music to study violin and piano after three years he became yet another composition pupil of Stanford. Bridge's route into the profession was as a practical performer, both on the viola and as conductor, available whenever a deputy was needed, a reputation he never entirely outgrew during forty years in the profession.

Later, Bridge was, of course, the composition teacher of the teenage Benjamin Britten, but he also left us a large catalogue of works which show radical stylistic development in the 1920s. Popular orchestral scores such as the suite *The Sea* failed to prepare public and critics for his rapprochement with the European avant-garde in the 1920s, and his reputation suffered. Almost forgotten as a composer for thirty years after his death, it was Benjamin Britten's revival of his late orchestral tone-poem *Enter Spring*, in 1966, and the activities of the Frank Bridge Trust in promoting his music, that led to the high reputation he enjoys today.

Bridge was profoundly depressed by the First World War, whose first personal blow for him came with the sinking of the *Lusitania* in June 1915. Immediately he composed his *Lament* for string orchestra in memory of 'Catherine, aged 9' who, with her family, was lost in the disaster. Increasingly the War appeared like a thread through his music and in 1916 he made this setting of Thomas à Kempis's meditation on inner peace as a commentary on the war. However, the words might well have appeared frankly pacifist during the conflict, and although the vocal score is dated March 1916, Bridge did not orchestrate it until October 1918. Published and performed almost immediately in 1919, it became a work of consolation, its intense hymn-like sentiments seeming a memorial for those lost in the War.

Thomas à Kempis's seven short verses are set with brief orchestral links between each, as the emotional intensity builds, the fifth being prefaced by a reprise of the opening words. In this work Bridge, not an habitual choral composer, seems to be taking his cue from his colleague Gustav Holst, with the long-running passages of flowing triads (heard first on flutes at the end of the short orchestral prelude). After the hushed peace of the opening verse the affirmative fast music of the second and third verses provides a first climactic point which runs on into a reprise of the opening words. But it is in the fourth verse where at the words 'love to be despised and not to be known in this world' Bridge achieved his moment of transcendent vision, where on a cymbal crash the music tries to tear itself from the tonality suggested by the note G playing in the bass. The vision fades and we are back with the second reprise of the opening words, the chorus fervently but softly asking 'that my heart may be at peace'. Now dividing into two choirs – in eight parts – the chorus maintain the note of quiet prayer and supplication to the radiant closing bars. The music ends on the single word 'Rest', and a vision of eternity, emotive music indeed in 1919.

LF

WILLIAM GILLIES WHITTAKER (1876-1944)
THE CŒLESTIAL SPHEARE
for chorus & orchestra

W G WHITTAKER WAS AN ENGLISH MUSIC SCHOLAR, CHORAL conductor and composer who studied science at Durham University. He then turned to music and joined the staff at Durham in 1898. In 1929 he was appointed as the first Gardiner Professor of Music at Glasgow University as well the first Principal of the Royal Scottish Academy of Music was made an Hon DMus of Durham University in 1921 and Edinburgh University in 1930. He resigned his post at the university in 1938, and from the Royal Scottish Academy in 1941.

He was particularly devoted to choral conducting and achieved fine results in Northumberland, especially with the Newcastle Bach Choir which he founded in 1915 to perform Bach cantatas in near-original conditions. He was a noted Bach scholar and was particularly keen to prepare performances of the cantatas in English translations. In 1927 he took the choir to Germany, where it toured with great success, performing Whittaker's own setting of Psalm 139 at the ISCM festival in Frankfurt-am-Main. In May 1924 the choir gave the first complete modern performance of Byrd's *Great Service* at Newcastle Cathedral, repeating it later at St Margaret's, Westminster, and in Oxford.

The Cœlestial Spheare was written whilst the composer was on a boat in the Indian Ocean between 10th and 20th July 1923. The orchestration was then completed in the South Pacific between 6th and 15th December 1923. One can easily imagine that the wonderful night sky, visible so much more clearly in the southern hemisphere, inspired the composer to set William Habington's mystical poem *The Cœlestial Spheare* to music. The work can be neatly viewed in three parts. The outer sections vividly convey the vast mysteriousness of the celestial sky

> **Nox nocti indicat Scientiam.** *David.*
> When I survey the bright
> Cœlestiall spheare:
> So rich with jewels hung, that night
> Doth like an Aethiop bride appear,
>
> My soule her wings doth spread
> And heaven-ward flies,
> Th'Almighty's mysteries to read
> In the large volumes of the skies.

whilst the dramatic middle section comments on the meaningless nature of time on earth when compared to the limitless expanse of time and space.

JG

FRÉDÉRIC D'ERLANGER (1868-1943)
MESSE DE REQUIEM
for soprano, alto, tenor, bass-baritone, chorus & orchestra

D'ERLANGER WAS BORN ON 29 MAY 1868 INTO A WEALTHY, aristocratic banking family. He was the third of four brothers born to an American mother and German father, Baron Frédéric Emil von Erlanger, who had founded Messrs Emil Erlanger & Co, an issuing house which arranged a loan for the Confederate forces during the American Civil War (1861-65). D'Erlanger's education was French, and he displayed considerable musical talent in his youth, particularly as a highly accomplished pianist. His great-nephew, Peter Denman, remembered the family home in Paris which included 'an enormous heavily furnished room with a large organ at one end, an organ that a friend of the family would play, sometimes as one of a duet improvising with a piano. I wish I could be sure that Freddy was the pianist – he liked improvising.'

When he was 20, d'Erlanger published his first book of songs. Soon after, the family company became Erlangers Ltd, merchant bankers in London, and the composer moved permanently to London, becoming a full-time banker with his elder brother Emile, and eventually taking British citizenship. Peter Denman: 'There was nothing "part-time" about Frederic as a banker. His elder brother took initiatives that sometimes needed restraint, a restraint that Frederic had no compunction in applying.'

D'Erlanger was a gentleman enthusiast in the old fashioned style, who used his wealth to pursue his passion for music and composition. 'He was a good pianist and occasionally gave recitals in public, sometimes including an improvisation. In his old age, and afflicted with tremors in both hands so that one wondered how he could possibly hit the right note, he managed without fail. He was on good terms with Adrian Boult and Barbirolli.' Lady Barbirolli writes. 'I do remember John talking about d'Erlanger, whom he knew and liked. I think that he conducted a work of d'Erlanger's in his first ever series of concerts in 1926 (aged 27), but I can't recall what the work was. It was so long before my time with John.' It is possible that this work was the orchestral waltz *Midnight Rose*, that Barbirolli recorded for HMV in 1934.

D'Erlanger enjoyed considerable success with his compositions. For example, the premiere of his Violin Concerto was given in 1903 by no less a fiddler than Fritz Kreisler. Apart from orchestral works, concerti and chamber music, d'Erlanger composed a number of operas and ballets that were performed at Covent Garden and throughout Europe. In 1906 his opera *Tess*, after Thomas Hardy's *Tess of the d'Urbervilles*, had its premiere at the San Carlo Theatre in Naples disrupted by an eruption of Vesuvius, and the theatre had to be evacuated. Three years later it was produced at Covent Garden starring Emmy Destinn and Giovanni Zenatello (and with Hardy in the audience), was repeated the following year and subsequently taken to Chemnitz and Budapest. The BBC broadcast the opera in 1929 from Daventry with Stiles Allen and Frank Titterton in the leads. His ballet, *Les Cent Baisers*, was produced at Covent Garden in 1935.

It was Adrian Boult who occasioned the first performances of the

The *appassionato* tenor solo in the 'Offertorium' of d'Erlanger's *Messe de Requiem* alluding to his opera *Tess*. (Reproduced with acknowledgement to theEstate of Frédéric d'Erlanger)

Messe de Requiem. In 1930 Boult left the Birmingham City Orchestra and Birmingham Festival Choral Society to take up his post as the BBC Music Director in London, and he became Chief Conductor of the BBC Symphony Orchestra the following year. In London, Boult became friends with d'Erlanger and agreed to premiere the *Requiem* over the wireless. The broadcast was transmitted from Daventry at 9.35 pm on Friday 27 February 1931, the soloists being Miriam Licette, Astra Desmond, Frank Titterton, and Keith Falkner (Boult was then 42). Boult's belief in d'Erlanger's *Requiem* prompted him to initiate its first public performance. For this he returned to his friends in Birmingham – his BFCS choir and the City of Birmingham Orchestra – and he conducted the work in Birmingham Town Hall on Wednesday 22nd March 1933 with soloists Maggie Teyte, Enid Cruickshank, Frank Titterton, and Keith Falkner (the programme also included the 'Good Friday Music' from Wagner's *Parsifal* and Parry's *Blest Pair of Sirens*). D'Erlanger attended this concert and 'was called to the platform and shared the plaudits with the performers'.

JP

GEORGE OLDROYD (1886-1951)
JHESU CHRIST, SAINT MARY'S SONE

for chorus & orchestra

OLDROYD WAS A YORKSHIREMAN, BUT HIS WORKING LIFE WAS spent in Surrey and London, mainly as composition teacher at Trinity College of Music, and as organist and choirmaster for 30 years at St Michael's, West Croydon. In the academic sphere his text hook *The Technique and Spirit of Fugue* (1948) was much respected, and the year before he died he was appointed King Edward VII Professor of Music in the University of London. Those who knew him describe him as quiet, scholarly, patient and gentle, and with great devotion to the Anglo-Catholic tradition of worship; 'spiritual yearning and a great sense of tonal beauty' were recognised in his lifetime as the characteristics of his music. He was dedicated to the harpsichord, at that time a considerable rarity, and his vocal works are much influenced by the modal scales of plainsong.

A typical climax in George Oldroyd's *Jhesu Christe,
Saint Mary's Sone* (Reproduced by permission of the
copyright owners Novello & Co.)

The present cantata was composed for the Croydon Triennial Musical Festival of 1931. The devotional words are by the 14th-century poet Richard Rolle of Hampole, and the scoring includes, along with all the instruments of the modern symphony orchestra, a major role for Oldroyd's beloved harpsichord, and a part for oboe d'amore. The melodies used are so steeped in a modal idiom that it is hard to tell where plainsong ends and original composition begins; and yet the harmonisation and the scoring are completely recognisable as of the first part of the 20th century.

A primary plainsong theme is that of the hymn *Jesu, dulcis memoria*, of which we hear the opening line played by oboe d'amore and violins in the orchestral introduction. The hymn tune is sung three times in full (beginning 'Jesu, thy love in to me send') at the opening of the second half of the cantata, and recurs as the basis for the exquisitely lovely final pages, where a three-part additional Choir of Angels weaves its seraphic Amens, above the serenely chanting chorus and delicate murmurings of the orchestra, to evoke a mood of the utmost spiritual ecstasy.

HO

BENJAMIN BRITTEN (1913-1976)
REJOICE IN THE LAMB, op 30
for soprano, alto, tenor & bass soli, chorus & organ

REJOICE IN THE LAMB HAS RIGHTLY FOUND A PLACE FOR ITSELF AT the centre of the choral repertoire. Since its commission in 1943 for the fiftieth anniversary of the consecration of St Matthew's Church, Northampton, the work has proved to be a popular favourite with both choirs and audiences everywhere; but its success is not difficult to fathom. It was Walter Hussey himself who suggested that Britten might set some of the bizarre words of the eighteenth century poet and visionary Christopher Smart, and these texts, with their flashes of genius and colourful imagery, immediately endear themselves to the listener. Onto this structure Britten lays some of his most immediately attractive writing – tuneful, rhythmic and emotionally wide-ranging. Always the most economical of composers, he manages to get quickly to the heart of the poetry, and the use of small, clearly defined musical ideas enables the listener to follow the progress of the music without difficulty through the succession of nine brief interlinked movements.

CB

Sir Lennox Berkeley (1903-1989)
FESTIVAL ANTHEM, op 21 no 2
for soprano & tenor, chorus & organ

BRITTEN'S *REJOICE IN THE LAMB*, FINZI'S *LO, THE FULL FINAL Sacrifice* and Bernstein's *Chichester Psalms* are just three of the many works which owe their creation to commissions from the Rev Walter Hussey. This remarkably far-sighted and cultured man supported and encouraged all branches of the Arts while rector of St Matthew's Church, Northampton, from the early 1940s and then while Dean of Chichester Cathedral during the 50s and 60s. He had an uncanny ability to point composers towards imaginative and wide-ranging texts that inspired works of the highest calibre. Amongst these is this undeservedly neglected work by Berkeley.

Apart from a handful of works the output of this fastidious composer remains largely unknown to the general musical public, yet his music has an expressive honesty and power which invariably repays closer study. His friendship with Benjamin Britten and a lifelong devotion to all things French (he was a pupil of Nadia Boulanger and a close friend of Poulenc) helped to mould a style which is marked by clarity of thought and structure, precisely imagined (and very personal) harmony and chording, and an often meltingly beautiful (though sometimes rather elusive) sense of melody. All these characteristics are present in the *Festival Anthem*. The text has an Easter theme, concerned with Death, Paradise and Resurrection, and the composer matches the colourful verbal imagery with vivid choral and solo vocal lines.

At the centre of the work's arch structure are gentle solos for soprano and tenor in the composer's most accessibly lyrical style, separated by a brief choral outburst describing the triumph of eternal life over death. The soprano solo (the first part of the piece to be composed) was clearly held in particular affection by Berkeley for he later transcribed it for cello and piano. In contrast the outer choral sections are more vigorous, marked by strong rhythms and idiosyncratically defined counterpoint and harmony. This is all underpinned by muscular organ writing that ranges from simple supportive harmony to elaborately patterned textures. The first performance took place in St. Matthew's Church, Northampton in 1945, and was broadcast later the same year in a programme that placed it alongside Britten's acclaimed masterpiece.

CB

GERALD FINZI (1901-1956)
LO! THE FULL, FINAL SACRIFICE
for chorus & organ

GERALD FINZI, WHO CAME FROM A WELL-OFF JEWISH FAMILY, whose cultural inheritance he repudiated, was self-consciously rooted in the English tradition, and his development was articulated through his love of English poetry which he set with a personal feeling for words and a melodic inflection that was uniquely his own. Finzi's lifelong love-affair with the English language (exemplified by his library, now preserved at Reading University) found expression in a long series of songs grouped in sets, and reflecting in particular his empathy with the poetry of Thomas Hardy. Finzi was a pupil of Ernest Farrar and had been deeply shocked by his teacher's death on the Western Front towards the end of the First World War, a loss which cast a shadow over his artistic life for many years. He subsequently studied with Sir Edward Bairstow at York, and later with R O Morris at the Royal College of Music.

Despite winning one of the publication prizes given by the Carnegie United Kingdom Trust in the 1920s, Finzi took some time to develop a distinctive style, and only in his thirties intuitively found his instantly recognisable personal voice arising from his word-setting, and response to the traditions of Elgar and Vaughan Williams but with a sympathy for a Bachian counterpoint and ebb and flow. Finzi also found landscape an inspiration, having a countryman's spirituality which, though agnostic as to creed, was characterised by a feeling which Stephen Banfield once referred to as 'personally unable to accept the Christian myth, he was nevertheless capable of wishing that its truth might be regenerated for him'.

After early years of loneliness Finzi achieved fruitful middle life through a deeply fulfilling marriage which encompassed a life of rural retreat. He felt that art could not be contrived and must find its own ace for a finished work to evolve. He portrayed the artistic life as being 'like a coral insect building his reef out of the transitory world around him and making a solid structure to last long after his own fragile and uncertain life'. His most celebrated work, *Dies Natalis*, a setting for solo voice and strings of words by the seventeenth century mystic Thomas Traherne, distils a childlike sense of wonder, and Finzi's settings span fourteen years. Life was indeed fragile for Finzi, who was diagnosed with leukaemia in 1949 and died in September 1956, while in full flood of composition.

Finzi wrote a succession of short choral works, and although he was habitually indecisive and slow in producing a finished score, *Lo! The Full, Final Sacrifice* was written to an urgent commission when the composer Alan Rawsthorne had failed to honour a deadline. This was for the Rev Walter Hussey, whose tenure of the living of St Matthews, Northampton, saw a significant celebration of the arts during and immediately after the Second World War. Probably best remembered for the fuss attendant on the unveiling of Henry Moore's sculpture 'Madonna and Child' in February 1944, his musical commissions included a succession of festival anthems, launched by Britten's *Rejoice in the Lamb* in 1943 followed by works by Edmund Rubbra, Lennox Berkeley and, in September 1946, Finzi's *Lo, The Full, Final Sacrifice* for the occasion of the 53rd anniversary of the consecration of the church. In 1947 the orchestral version was first heard at the Three Choirs Festival, which that year was held at Gloucester.

In evoking the liturgical drama of the Eucharist, Finzi took as his text verses from Richard Crashaw (1612-1649), using versions of two consecutive 'Hymns of St Thomas Aquinas in adoration of the Blessed Sacrament' – *Adoro Te* and *Lauda Sion Salvatorem* – in Crashaw's collection *Carmen Deo Nostro*, which, in fact, had not been first published, in Paris, until three years after Crashaw's death.

The two texts were closely mixed by Finzi, producing a composite poem. The opening three verses are the last from 'Lauda Sion', though with the omission of two lines; we then have six of the eight lines of the fifth verse of 'Adoro Te' ending with the words 'my surer self to me'. There follow the two opening verses of 'Lauda Sion' and we end with the last 12-line verse of 'Adoro Te'. Thus we have a text which in its expression Finzi made his own in his disposition of Crashaw's baroque imagery. This is underlined by the composer's glowing, ecstatic setting, finding a mood of almost transcendental affirmation, perfectly caught by Finzi's idiosyncratic fusion of imagery and music. Finzi's seemingly effortless flowing lines, his hushed sense of expectation, and vibrant central climax at the words 'This sovereign subject . . . provokes thy praise', revealing a personal resource familiar to lovers of *Dies Natalis* and much else besides.

LF

CHRISTOPHER LE FLEMING (1908-1985)
FIVE PSALMS
for soprano, chorus & orchestra

---

1 *Psalm 120 'When I was in trouble'* (chorus)
2 *Psalm 121 'I will life up mine eyes'* (chorus)
3 *Psalm 23 'The Lord is My Shepherd'* (solo)
4 *Psalm 107 'They that go down to the sea in ships'* (solo & chorus)
5 *Psalm 150 'O Praise God in His Holiness'* (solo and chorus)

VERY MUCH OF THE GENERATION AND SYMPATHIES OF GERALD FINZI, with whom he was often a house guest, Christopher Le Fleming was born in Wimborne, Dorset, and despite his great personal interest when young, entered music fairly late owing to an eye complaint. Although largely self-taught he attended the Brighton School of Music, studied piano with George Reeves, and later found himself within the orbit of Vaughan Williams, as may be heard from his music. His first published music came when he was 21, with a unison setting of Eleanor Farjeon's *Cradle Song for Christmas*.

There followed songs and piano pieces, and music for schools including a light opera *Penelope Anne*. Later came a number of short choral works, of which tonight's music is a typical example, a *Suite for Strings* and a characteristic evocation of the English countryside, *Bramshaw Folly*, for piano and strings. Le Fleming was notably associated with music education, particularly at the Rural Music Schools Association, the Royal School of Church Music and many freelance teaching posts. He also became the Chairman of the Composer's Guild and became well-known among his colleagues as a champion of the professional composer. He died in Woodbury, Devon on 19 June 1985.

Le Fleming's *Five Psalms*, designated as 'Opus 10' (though not on the printed copies) were written in 1939 but not heard owing to the war.

Their first performance came at the Gloucester Three Choirs in 1947 when the celebrated soprano Elsie Suddaby was the soloist. In the same festival was heard the first performance of the orchestral version of Finzi's *Lo! the Full Final Sacrifice*. Later Vaughan Williams chose Le Fleming's *Five Psalms* for the Leith Hill Music Festival.

In his treatment of the music, Le Fleming's gradually develops his treatment across the set, to the crowning affirmation of the 150th Psalm for soloist, chorus and orchestra in the fifth movement. After the choral climax of the opening 120th Psalm, the semi-chorus sing the well-known words 'I will lift up mine eyes into the hills' (Psalm 121), the whole setting in only two parts, with the men and women each in unison. The flowing 12/8 centre piece is a radiant but straightforward treatment of 'The Lord is My Shepherd' – the 23rd Psalm – introducing the soprano soloist. The movement is dedicated to the memory of Alfred Tanner. Le Fleming's wife was Phyllis Tanner and one assumes this movement is dedicated to her brother or father. The fourth movement, which one critic saw as 'a maiden watching the departure of the ships carrying to distant lands her sailor lover', takes two familiar verses (vv 23-4) from Psalm 107, 'They that go down to the sea in ships', but presents them in an individual, fervent, unexpectedly slow setting, rising to commanding climaxes, preceded by a singing introduction of quietly flowing contrapuntal lines.

Le Fleming saves his grand statement for the closing setting of 'Praise God in His Holiness', the 150th Psalm. Here the celebratory, optimistic mood is evoked with fanfaring motifs, and the first climax by the use of the 'alleluias' from a familiar melody from the *Cölner Gesangbuch* of 1623, which we know as the hymn 'All Creatures of Our God and King'.

LF

WILLIAM LLOYD WEBBER (1914-1982)
DIVINE COMPASSION
for soprano, tenor, chorus & orchestra

WILLIAM LLOYD WEBBER WAS BORN INTO A POOR LONDON FAMILY IN 1914. His father was a self-employed plumber, who was also a keen organ 'buff'. William started to play the organ himself and by the age of 14 he had already become a well-known organ recitalist, giving frequent performances at many important churches and cathedrals throughout Great Britain. He studied composition with Ralph Vaughan Williams at the Royal College of Music, where he gained his RCO diploma at the age of nineteen.

The years immediately following the Second World War saw the birth of his two sons, Andrew and Julian, and also the beginning of Lloyd Webber's most prolific years as a composer. It was during these years that he wrote *Divine Compassion.*

Lloyd Webber's roots were firmly embedded in the romanticism of such composers as Rachmaninov, Sibelius and Franck, and he became increasingly convinced that his own music was 'out of step' with the prevailing climate of the time. Rather than compromise his style, he turned to the academic side of British musical life – teaching at the Royal College of Music and, in 1964, accepting the Directorship of the London College of Music. Disillusioned with composition, he wrote virtually nothing for the next 20 years – until shortly before his death, when he began composing again.

His music has remained virtually undiscovered until recently when works that have lain unpublished and unperformed for many years have gradually come to light. Today in an age when the musical world is perhaps more ready to accept new compositions in many different styles, we can listen to William Lloyd Webber's music as if for the first time.

Divine Compassion is a Cantata based on the Gospel according to St John. It is in three parts. The first part tells the story of Jesus's early ministry. The second focuses on the passion story and the third on the first Easter Day. Tonight, we will be performing the first two parts only.

Divine Compassion is a very skilfully crafted work with plenty of memorable melodic lines and persuasive harmonies. Lloyd Webber uses recurrent themes to illustrate the central theme of glory in sacrifice. For instance, the same harmonies are used to depict Jesus 'giving up the ghost' as those used at the end of the 'Love of Christ' movement, finishing with the words 'eternal glory shall surround thy head'.

This use of themes is almost Wagnerian. The crowd shouting for Christ to be crucified have a theme, repeating frequently during Jesus's trial. The two choruses, *Christ Betrayed* and the *Condemnation of Christ,* are set to the same music to illustrate human complicity in the crucifixion.

The structure of the piece is along similar lines to Stainer's *Crucifixion,* with hymns at the end of each part and two soloists, a tenor Evangelist and a bass Jesus. The chorus have two main roles. Firstly, to comment on the action that has just taken place and secondly, to represent the crowd in the passion scenes leading up to the crucifixion.

Divine Compassion – Part 1

THE GLORY INCARNATE (Evangelist, Chorus, Jesus). *Divine Compassion* starts with the opening verses of St John's Gospel, 'In the beginning was the word' sung by the evangelist. The chorus then introduce one of the central themes of the work – 'the glory of the word of God eternal'. The next passage has Jesus's first words, 'The hour is come, that the Son of Man should be glorified'. The last part contains an extended section for the evangelist likening the life of Jesus to a grain of wheat that dies and then 'tip-springs a life to feed the hungry multitude'.

CHRIST THE BREAD OF LIFE (Jesus, Chorus). Jesus explains to the people the answer to their question 'How can this man give us his flesh to eat?'

CHRIST, THE GOOD SHEPHERD (Jesus). Jesus sings 'I am the good shepherd; the good shepherd lays down his life for the sheep'.

ADORATION OF CHRIST, THE FAITHFUL SHEPHERD (Sopranos and Altos of the Chorus, Evangelist). There follows a delightful duet showing Lloyd Webber's melodic ability to the full. The Evangelist then ends the section with a heroic 'He loved them unto the end'.

THE LOVE OF CHRIST (Chorus). The theme of enduring love is taken up by the chorus.

THE HIGH-PRIESTLY INTERCESSION (Jesus). Jesus prays to the father 'that the love wherewith thou hast loved me may be in them and I in them'.

THE CHRISTIAN SOUL'S RESPONSE TO CHRIST'S PRAYER (Hymn sung by Chorus). A unison hymn in 4 verses entitled 'Jesu, divine intercessor'.

Part 2

THE GLORY OF SACRIFICE (Evangelist). This marks the beginning of the passion story. We are introduced to Judas, the betrayer of Jesus.

CHRIST BETRAYED (Chorus). This unaccompanied chorus notes that all who 'scorn thy love' and 'betray thy name', 'share the traitor Judas's fall'.

THE ARREST (Evangelist, Jesus, Tenors and Basses of the Chorus). The movement begins with a menacing theme in the organ to denote Jesus' impending arrest. The chorus identify whom they are seeking. The bare chords of 'Jesus of Nazareth' leave the listener in no doubt.

CHRIST IN THE HANDS OF HIS ENEMIES (Chorus). This is a remarkable movement beginning with a slow march-like theme, 'Where is the word which once the worlds created?' and ending with an optimistic section in a major key depicting Christ going 'to conquer in his final fight'.

PETER'S DENIAL OF CHRIST (Evangelist, Damsel, Peter, Chorus, a servant). Peter denies Jesus three times and 'immediately the cock crew'.

CHRIST DENIED BY HIS FRIEND (Tenors and Basses of the Chorus, Evangelist). This movement echoes the feelings of Peter after his denial of Jesus – 'O proud heart, low thou'rt fallen'. However the Evangelist joins the chorus with a reassuring message that 'thy compassion and thy faith can make these proud weak hearts, strong'.

CHRIST BEFORE PILATE (Evangelist, Pilate, Chorus of Jews, Jesus). Pilate questions the chorus of Jews and Jesus himself on the case against Jesus.

CHRIST JUDGED BY WORLDLY POWER (Evangelist and Chorus). The Evangelist takes a step back from the action to ask 'Art thou a king?' The chorus join him as he answers in the affirmative. The movement ends with a daring harmonic turn to be repeated when Jesus 'gives up the ghost' later in the work.

CHRIST MOCKED AND CONDEMNED (Evangelist, Chorus of Soldiers, Jews and Chief Priests, Pilate, Jesus). The organ theme from the 'Christ before Pilate' section returns as Jesus is finally condemned to be crucified.

THE CONDEMNATION OF CHRIST (Chorus). The music from 'Christ betrayed' returns as the chorus sing of sharing the blame for the events. 'But low in penitence we bow, for we too crucified our Lord, and share the grievous blame'.

CHRIST CRUCIFIED (Evangelist, Chorus of Soldiers, Jesus). The final moments from Jesus's life are described.

THE GLORY OF THE CRUCIFIED (Hymn sung by Chorus). Part 2 ends in a similar way to part 1 with a hymn. The writer asks 'Was there no glory in that hour when on the cross our Saviour died?' Through the 5 verses, we learn of the glory of the crucified.

DG

GERALD FINZI (1901-1956)
INTIMATIONS OF IMMORTALITY
for tenor, chorus & orchestra

LIKE ELGAR'S *THE DREAM OF GERONTIUS*, AND UNLIKE BRITTEN'S *Spring Symphony*, Finzi's *Intimations of Immortality* is a continuous setting of one long poem. He completed it for the 1950 Gloucester Three Choirs Festival; Herbert Sumsion conducted and the soloist was Eric Greene. But he had begun work on it before the 1939-45 war, probably with no specific thought of a Three Choirs production. He was, however, a regular and keen attender of these Festivals, and his *Dies Natalis* should have had its first performance at the cancelled 1939 Festival.

Finzi admitted that he was 'driven to compose' this work 'by the impact of the words'. He knew that he risked being criticised for setting a poem which, as he said, 'both in its philosophic content and poetic expression is one of the greatest in the English language'. In 1936 he had published two of Milton's best-known sonnets for tenor and small orchestra, and had been charged 'with attempting a task which he should not have set himself'. The essence of this criticism was not so much that Milton's verse was too fine, or too famous, but that, expressing abstract thought, it imposed particular problems for a composer. Finzi's spirited reaction was that 'the first and last thing is that a composer is (presumably) moved by a poem and wishes to identify himself with it and share it'.

It was perhaps predictable that anyone who had set Thomas Traherne, as Finzi did so memorably in *Dies Natalis*, should come to compose *Intimations of Immortality from recollections of early childhood* – so runs the full title of Wordsworth's Ode. Finzi shared with the two poets the view of infancy as a blessed state, when the untrammelled child is filled with wonder and sees the world in a 'celestial light'; his own lifelong concern was to keep this vision fresh when custom and responsibilities began to press. It would be naive to suppose that Finzi took this view too literally; the child's fresh vision must stand for the artist's vision, which has to be held clear and singly through the daily adult round. But he did always place a higher value on intuition and perception than on experience, and at home in his music-making he gave young people a special welcome and warmly fostered their talents.

For all Finzi's justification, the Ode does pose problems for a composer. It is entirely descriptive and reflective, with no dialogue, and no dramatic events. There is a narrator who at times speaks personally and at others as a commentator. Finzi might have reserved the soloist for the individual 'I' and the chorus for the philosophic 'we'. But he does not; for instance, 'to me alone there came a thought of grief' is sung by the chorus without sopranos, which suggests that he was more concerned with finding the right colour for a train of thought than with making an analytical, schematic division of the text.

Wordsworth continually shifts his perspective of time, comparing *then* with *now*, relating past glory to present loss, or balancing present against past beauty, half-remembered. So the composer is challenged to hold remembered glory and the current sense of exile from it, at one and the same moment. Music has no tenses, but it has its own means of recall. The solo horn call which opens the work rises as if from a treasured past; it is transformed to a funeral march for 'Our birth is but a sleep', in a striking reversal of conventional thinking; and it sounds magically, now in the major, on two occasions as the soloist refers to pre-existence as the perfect standard that human life aspires to. Finzi writes in a late romantic style, rich in melancholy, with also a spring of pure lyric melody, in which he rises to the natural delights and to the ambivalent bitter-sweet climaxes of Wordsworth's Ode.

DMV

Ralph Vaughan Williams (1872-1958)
PILGRIM'S JOURNEY
(adapted by Christopher Morris & Roy Douglas)
for soprano, tenor, chorus & orchestra

1. *Cast Thy Burden Upon the Lord*
2. *Into Thy Hands O Lord*
3. *Who would true valour see*
4. *Unto Him That Overcometh*
5. *Vanity Fair*
6. *He That is Down*
7. *The Lord is My Shepherd*
8. *Alleluia*

THE SON OF THE VICAR OF DOWN AMPNEY, GLOUCESTERSHIRE, who died when the future composer was only three, Ralph Vaughan Williams was the grandson of Sir Edward Vaughan Williams, a celebrated judge, on his father's side, and Josiah Wedgewood on his mother's, and was also related to Charles Darwin. Vaughan Williams thus grew up at Leith Hill Place near Dorking, Surrey, where his mother had returned to her family. Incidentally we have tended to associate Vaughan Williams with the 'coloured counties' of Worcester, Gloucester and Shropshire, but one only has to visit Leith Hill Place in its elevated position on Leith Hill, to realise that the future composer grew up with the panorama of Surrey and distant Sussex daily spread before him.

Perhaps we have tended to have a rather homespun idea of Vaughan Williams, and one gets the feeling he was not unhappy with the image. In fact he was a highly educated, musically experienced, and remarkably sophisticated artist. His education at Charterhouse and Cambridge was that of a leader both intellectual and artistic. His Cambridge degree was in history and as well as being a pupil of Parry and Stanford at the Royal College of Music he studied widely, not only with English teachers such as Charles Wood and Alan Gray, but also on the continent with Max Bruch and later with Ravel. Folksong collector, editor of *The English Hymnal* and later *Songs of Praise*, editor of Purcell, organist and conductor, he, whether consciously or unconsciously, managed a synthesis of what we now see as archetypal national elements.

Although he took longer than many to acquire his mature voice, the progress of his music over an active life spanning more than 60 years is quite remarkable, yet always informed by his personal voice and with something distinctive and arresting to say. He wrote in every genre from songs to opera, choral music to symphonies, chamber music to ballet. His enormous integrity and liberal humanist spirit in the tradition of Sir Hubert Parry, his mentor, gave him a commanding position in our music. Vaughan Williams was a product of his times, but he also transcended them by developing a musical language to which a wide spectrum of music lovers could respond. As Michael Kennedy has remarked: 'its appeal at several levels makes it a remarkable expression of the national spirit in music'.

In no work do we enjoy music that spans his career more than in *The Pilgrim's Progress*. Vaughan Williams first wrote for *The Pilgrim's Progress* when asked for incidental music for a local staging of Bunyan's allegory at Reigate in 1906. Thus was started a life-long preoccupation with Bunyan's book which subsequently found expression in the 'pastoral episode' *The Shepherds of the Delectable Mountains*, a one act chamber opera, first performed in 1922, which was later assimilated into the final act of his final setting of Bunyan's allegory. In 1942 the BBC broadcast a radio version made by Edward Sackville-West, for which Vaughan Williams produced an extended score, more recently recast by the late Christopher Palmer for modern performance. Soon after there appeared the composer's Fifth Symphony, written between 1938 and 1943 and first heard in June 1943, which included thematic material from the later stage work, notably the twelve bars from the opening of the scene at the House Beautiful. Vaughan Williams always called his staging of Bunyan 'A Morality', and it was first seen at the Royal Opera House Covent Garden in April 1951. The composer refused to allow church or concert performance of the complete score, but after his death, Christopher Morris and Roy Douglas prepared *Pilgrim's Journey*, featuring highlights of the stage work, which was approved by Ursula Vaughan Williams on the grounds that the composer himself had endorsed similar concert scores from his earlier operas. The result of their labours was first heard at the Leith Hill Festival at the composer's home town of Dorking in April 1963.

The extracts, which follow the chronology of the complete score, are largely self-explanatory. The first opens with the hymn tune 'York', immediately followed by a rising motif which, in fact, comes from his *Tallis Fantasia* of forty years before, all that remains of music that was more extensively associated with RVW's earlier versions of

Bunyan. This leads into the music Vaughan Williams wrote for the Three Shining Ones in Act I scene ii as Pilgrim, kneeling, pleads to be saved, and (moving forward a little) the Interpreter sings 'An open door shall be set before thee'. In the cantata the music follows the sequence of the complete music of *Pilgrim's Progress* and moves with a pause into the second number. Here 'Into Thy Hands O Lord' is the Nocturne, the optional Intermezzo between Acts I and II sung by Watchful, the Porter by the Wicket Gate into the grounds of the House Beautiful. It is followed by the hymn 'Who would true valour see' the linking narrative omitted in the cantata in the interest of a choral opening, before the herald announces that 'the night is far spent'.

There follows an interlude as the women's voices sing 'Unto him that overcometh' where we find Pilgrim exhausted after he has slain Apollyon at the end of Act II; he is here addressed by two Heavenly Beings, the Branch Bearer (bearing a branch of the Tree of Life) and the Cup Bearer (with a cup of the Water of Life). Having greeted him they sprinkle water on his forehead and anoint him with leaves, taking off his helmet and breastplate. This provides a striking contrast to the vivid scherzo evoking Vanity Fair, where we are given much of the opening music seen in Act III scene i on the stage. 'He that is down' is sung by the Woodcutter's Boy at the beginning of the fourth act; the boy is sitting chopping fire-wood as Pilgrim approaches remarking 'I dare to say he leads a merrier life and wears more of the herb called Heart's-ease in his bosom than he that is clad in silk and velvet'. The Delectable Mountains are now visible in the far distance. Here it is given the briefest treatment, yet is surely one of the most striking tunes in the whole work.

The cantata ends with the celebratory 'Alleluias' as Pilgrim reaches the end of his journey. There is no particular need to place the separate movements of *Pilgrim's Journey* as they are found in the parent work, but I hope it gives some context to those who may not have heard it before. The work is available in optional versions reduced orchestra including one for strings, two pianos and organ, trumpet and percussion.

LF

EDMUND RUBBRA (1902-1986)
SONG OF THE SOUL
for chorus & orchestra

EDMUND RUBBRA'S FATHER WORKED IN A SHOE FACTORY IN Northampton, and Rubbra went out to work at the age of 14 as a railway booking clerk. But he studied music from an early age, and as a pianist his enthusiasm for the music of Cyril Scott led him to put on a local concert of Scott's music in Northampton Public Library, as a result of which Scott offered him composition lessons. Thanks to his travel pass as a railway employee, Rubbra was able to accept. Later he studied with Holst at Reading University and at the Royal College of Music. He emerged as a pianist, musical journalist and composer, and he told me he was always able to support himself through music. He later became a celebrated teacher both at Oxford and at the Guildhall School of Music.

First known for his second Violin Sonata and songs, Rubbra won much acclaim for his eleven symphonies, many of which were performed at the Proms. He also wrote vocal music throughout his life.

Rubbra first looked to the sixteenth-century Spanish mystic St John of the Cross, a contemporary of El Greco, for his choral setting *The Dark Night of the Soul*, completed in 1942. Ten years later in *Song of the Soul* Rubbra turned to him again, this time in the English translation by Roy Campbell. Commissioned by the London Bach Society, the work appeared in 1953.

Here the key to Rubbra's setting comes with the subtitle printed in the vocal score: 'in intimate communication and union with the love of God'. From the outset, in this short, but intense, musical vision, the composer establishes a mystical mood, quickly building a typically subtle evocation in sensuous musical terms, ardently reflecting the poet's fusion of religious fervour in the language of earthly love. The harp is particularly important in colouring the texture with an illumination that reflects the words.

We need to note how, in the first five bars, Rubbra uses a simple motif which gently rises and falls and then inverts, the answering fragments informing much of the composer's invention. The music's ambiguous tonality and subtly shifting harmonies underline the poet's quest until the fervour of Rubbra's final setting of 'In glory, grace and rest', when the orchestra, finally fortissimo, play the opening motif now triumphant.

LF

Sir George Dyson (1883-1964)
AGINCOURT
cantata for chorus and orchestra

In a generation when many of the leading British composers were well-off, often with allowances and private incomes, it is good to remember that Sir George Dyson, doyen of public school music and the Director of the Royal College of Music, in fact came from a working class background in the north of England. He was an entirely a self-made man.

Dyson was first an organist. In his autobiography he remembered playing for church services at the age of thirteen, and by the time he was 16 he was a Fellow of the Royal College of Organists. Thus he became an open scholar at the Royal College of Music, coming to London in 1900 as a pupil of Stanford. Dyson studied at the Royal College for four years eventually winning a Mendelssohn scholarship which allowed him to travel on the continent. On Stanford's advice he chose Italy where he encountered the then leading Italian orchestral composers: Buonamici, Sgambati and Martucci. He also spent some time in Vienna, in Berlin and in Dresden. He thus met many of the leading musicians of the day, including Richard Strauss, and Joachim. Later, in London, Nikisch produced his early Straussian symphonic poem evoking the Palio, which he called *Siena*, though unfortunately the music does not survive.

He returned to London in 1907. At 24, this working class boy from industrial Halifax had acquired an enviable musical technique, and a patina of the genteel man-about-Europe. But he needed to earn his living, and Sir Hubert Parry recommended him to be music master at Osborne, the Royal Naval College, and from there it was but a step to Marlborough College, and after three years, to Rugby.

Joining up on the outbreak of war, he wrote a *Manual of Grenade Fighting* later widely circulated as *Grenade Warfare*. Shell-shocked in 1916, he eventually found himself working in the Air Ministry where he helped establish RAF bands, and he also realised the march *RAF March Past* that Sir Walford Davies had sketched in short score. In 1920 Dyson's *Three Rhapsodies* for string quartet, composed soon after his return from the continent before the war, were chosen for publication under the Carnegie UK Trust's publication scheme, thus drawing attention to him as a rising young composer, though at that stage with few substantial works to his name. To crown his achievement and the return to normality, he was appointed to Wellington College, and he also became a professor at the Royal College of Music. It was at this time that he produced his celebrated book *The New Music*, published in 1924, and widely admired in its day for its learning and apparently commonsense view.

The most productive part of Dyson's life as a composer came while he was Director of Music at Winchester College, an appointment he held from 1924 to 1937. Here not only was he organist, but he had a choir and an orchestra for concerts, as well as an adult choral society. If one said that he composed as a hobby, one would give quite the wrong idea. Yet this was a spare time activity in a busy professional life of teaching, lecturing and performing. He first achieved his most characteristic voice with choral music of a tuneful vigorous cast. Choral societies responded from the first, and *In Honour of the City* (1928) and three years later *The Canterbury Pilgrims* established him as a vibrant musical personality of some stature. *The Canterbury Pilgrims* enjoyed a wide but short-lived success with choral societies round the English speaking world.

Dyson became associated with the Three Choirs Festival and produced several choral works for them, including the now neglected *St Paul's Voyage to Melita* in 1933, *Nebuchadnezzar* in 1935 and the more spiritual *Quo Vadis?*, not performed complete until 1949. Other works included the Symphony in G (1937) and the Violin Concerto (1941). Other vocal music followed including *Sweet Thames Run Softly*, a mellifluous setting for baritone, chorus and orchestra of words from Edmund Spenser's *Prothalamion*, which in 1955 was thought a backward-looking idiom. It was at first well-received, but was soon forgotten in the avant-garde 1960s.

Finally came the 20-minute nativity sequence *A Christmas Garland*, and the work we hear tonight, *Agincourt*. For this short brilliant choral setting, written for the Jubilee of the Petersfield Music Festival in 1956, Dyson assembled a jigsaw of familiar words selected from Shakespeare's *Henry V*. He ended with a favourite fifteenth century setting he had pioneered between the wars, the *Hymn after Agincourt* (1415), which by the 1950s was well-known following Walton's use of it in his *Henry V* film music.

Dyson breaks his text into six contrasted sections. These mini-movements are each given a new character by short orchestral introductions. In the fifth Dyson elides words from the scene of the night before the battle, with the very well-known 'St Crispin's Day' speech, the men taking the words of the king, contrasted with the women who given a narrative tone to those parts of the speech which set the scene. At the end all come together for the finale, and the rousing and patriotic closing bars, almost as if this was Dyson's personal thanksgiving for victory in 1945, as well as in 1415.

LF

Benjamin Britten (1913-1976)
CANTATA ACADEMICA, CARMEN BASILIENSE, op 62
for soprano, tenor, alto & bass, chorus & orchestra

PART 1
1. *Corale* (G)
2. *Alla Rovescio* (F)
3. *Recitativo* (Eb/D#)
4. *Arioso* (E)
5. *Duettino* (F#)
6. *Recitativo* (A)
7. *Scherzo* (D - Bb - D)

PART 2
8. *Tema Seriale con fuga*
9. *Soli e Duettino* (C)
10.*Ariosocon Canto Populare* (Db)
11.*Recitativo* (B)
12.*Canone ed ostinato* (G#)
13.*Corale con canto* (G)

All three composers on our programme tonight developed early, and had become precocious young composers in their teens. Benjamin Britten first emerged for the wider audience when he was nineteen with the choral variations *A Boy Was Born*. However, in the years up to the war, Britten in his early and mid twenties was seen by his admirers as 'clever', even brittle, in works such as the *Variations on a Theme of Frank Bridge*, the Piano Concerto and the song cycle *Our Hunting Fathers*. His departure for America in 1939 meant that he was removed from the musical scene at home during the early years of the war. His return in 1942, his subsequent touring with Peter Pears (especially with his folksong arrangements), the performance of the *Sinfonia da Requiem*, the *Serenade for tenor, horn and strings* and finally *Peter Grimes* established him as a major figure. This was reinforced by the works that followed including the *Spring Symphony*, the *St Nicholas* cantata and the operas *The Rape of Lucretia* and *Albert Herring*. Britten was now widely seen as a composer particularly associated with the voice.

To his admirers at the time, the late 1950s was something of a crossroads in the music of Benjamin Britten. The opera *A Midsummer Night's Dream* and *A War Requiem*, were yet to appear and briefly he appeared to have lost some of his earlier impetus. The *Nocturne* and the children's cantata *Noye's Fludde* were really his last widely played works at the time, the ballet *The Prince of the Pagodas* seemed to present a new face to a composer which would not be assimilated for some years.

Thus with the wider public, Britten's reputation was largely dependent on his sensitive settings of English poetry, idiomatically – and idiosyncratically – performed by Peter Pears, and other singers associated with the composer. The exuberant score we hear tonight is demonstrably Britten in his most inventive and characteristic mood. Yet this work, written for the 500th anniversary of Basel University, and first performed there on 1 July 1960 under the baton of Paul Sacher, finds Britten, that superb setter of words, writing a choral work, setting a text in Latin. Here arguably articulating the actual words is of little interest to most of the audiences, for Britten's celebratory and joyous setting succeeds entirely on its own account, almost independently of the words. Recorded soon after the first performance, and first heard in Britain on 10 March 1961, it has never achieved the wide audience of Britten's other choral works despite the music's sure popular touch. Its individual moments are very much in the mould that made the *Spring Symphony* so popular, but without that work's evocative texts.

The Latin text was compiled by Bernard Wyss from the university charter and contemporary texts in praise of the City of Basel. Britten took this ceremonial text and set it in ten movements linked by three recitatives, the whole falling into two parts. Written at a time when the twelve tone technique of Arnold Schoenberg predominated, at least in academic and avant-garde circles, Britten's theme, on which the whole work is based, uses all twelve tones of the chromatic scale, but makes a considerable point by using them tonally. As this is a work to celebrate an academic institution each movement is built on a different musical device, such as canon or fugue, and done so in a completely structured way. The theme is G, F, Eb, E, F#, A, D, Bb, C, Db, Cb. Ab, and each movement is based on a different note of the 'thema' in that order, although the theme is only ever heard complete in the eighth movement at the beginning of Part 2. The total effect is thus ultimately light-hearted but it encompasses all Britten's most deeply felt musical tricks and techniques of the time, and one is ambivalent whether he meant us to take them at face value or with any measure of irony.

The mood is set by the brilliant opening fanfares and the chorus's celebratory 'corale'. The second movement takes both Britten's lyrical agenda in dealing with his text, and the strict academicism of his manner, as he presents a canon by inversion, the men's stirringly lyrical invention soon answered by the women with the tune inverted, each responding ever quicker until they sing together. There follows the first recitative announced by the piano, a sequence of florid decoration for the tenor, and soon launching the bass soloist and then the soprano and contralto in duet. Finally the tenor returns with the second recitativo, a typically agile Brittenesque passage written for Peter Pears's voice, and the first half ends with all four soloists and the chorus in an exhilarating swinging fugal scherzo with a dramatic contrasting middle section.

At the beginning of the second part we hear the theme for the first time, presented as a solemn and expressive chorale, followed by a brilliant fugue in which each entry starts on the successive notes of the theme. The theme finally returns and quickly leads to the ninth movement in which, reflecting the second movement, we have arias by the bass and alto soloists, the first abrupt and dramatic the second flowing, which then combine. The tenth movement is possibly the gorgeous soft centre of the work: as the soprano floats an exquisite high-lying line (perhaps bringing to mind 'Out on the lawn' in the *Spring Symphony*) accompanied by high strings and harp, the sound of the men steals in as from afar, humming a popular Swiss students' song, the whole confection strongly reminiscent of the *Spring Symphony*. The tenor and piano now return with his third recitative, leading to the two connected movements which together form the work's finale. In the twelfth movement, soloists and punchy brass set up a brilliant counterpoint with the chorus, the raucous choral climax over an orchestral ostinato driven on by the side drum and orchestra. It broadens into the celebratory last movement in which the opening Corale returns, and the 'student song' from the tenth movement appears as a descant on piano and bells, bring the music to a brilliant close.

LF

JOHN JOUBERT (b 1927)
THE CHOIR INVISIBLE, op 54
a choral symphony for baritone, chorus & orchestra

I *Let us now praise famous men* (Ecclesiasticus 44vv. 1-15)

II *I think continually of those who were truly great* (Stephen Spender)
III *O may I join the choir invisible* (George Eliot)

BORN ON 29 MARCH 1927, IN CAPE TOWN, SOUTH AFRICA, JOHN JOUBERT received his earliest musical education in Cape Town but moved to Britain in 1946 as the result of the award of a Performing Right Society Scholarship to the Royal Academy of Music, London. Here he studied with Theodore Holland and Howard Ferguson. In 1950 he was appointed as a music lecturer at the University of Hull. Since 1962 Joubert has lived in Birmingham, where he held the post of reader in music at the University. In 1979 he was visiting professor at the University of Otago, New Zealand. He decided in 1986 to take early retirement in order to devote more time to composition though his distinguished academic career had not hindered his activity as a composer of impressive stature.

Notable amongst the early works is the Violin Concerto of 1954 premiered at the York Festival. He has written some notable operas; *In the Drought* (1956), *Silas Marner* (1961), *The Quarry* (1965), *Under Western Eyes* (1968) with the latter making a strong impression at the 1969 Camden Festival.

As his opera subjects suggest, he regards the composer as responsible to society as well as to art. In his writings he has expressed opinions on many subjects embracing political, religious and liturgical ideas besides those dealing directly with musical matters. The music has immediate appeal and yet continues to satisfy when subjected to closer analysis.

The Choir Invisible was written to celebrate the 150th anniversary of the Halifax Choral Society and subsequently was premiered by them, with the baritone Thomas Hemsley and the Royal Liverpool Philharmonic Orchestra, under the composer's baton, on 18 May 1968. The three movements of *The Choir Invisible* run without a break.

The first opens in grand style with a paean of praise to our heroic forefathers. This mood is contrasted with a passage that hauntingly reminds us that many have '*no memorial* despite their *righteousness*'. But the music slowly builds in hope as the chorus sings: 'their seed shall remain for ever'. Again the music dissolves away into uncertainty for the lines: 'Their bodies are buried in peace; but their name liveth for evermore' only for a theme of hope, previously introduced to the words 'such as found out musical tunes' to lead us up to the final climax of the movement.

The middle movement is for the baritone soloist and orchestra alone. Here there is a more operatic feel to the word setting with recitative-like musings from the soloist gradually developing into more and more lyrical lines that rise to the powerful final line of the poem 'And left the vivid air signed with their honour'.

The third and final movement begins with a dark and solemn funeral march: 'O may I join the choir invisible Of those immortal dead who live again.' Slowly rays of light appear – *'thoughts sublime'* – *'so to live is heaven'* and it is this latter line that sees the reappearance of the 'hope' theme. There is still much soul-searching to be undertaken before the music begins its long gradual ascent into the heavens and the reprise of the opening musical ideas in the work's exultant climax.

JG

JOHN JOUBERT (b 1927)
FOR THE BEAUTY OF THE EARTH
a choral symphony for baritone, chorus & orchestra

Communication is important to me. I want to he understood enjoyed and used. I do not want to live in the enclosed and artificial world of 'Contemporary Music'; but in the repertory of musicians whom I respect, in the schools, in the churches, and in the theatre. I also have a profound respect for the musical culture of amateurs and with this very important section of the musical public I have enjoyed some of my most rewarding musical experiences. – John Joubert

BORN IN CAPE TOWN, SOUTH AFRICA, OF HUGUENOT LINEAGE, John went to an Anglican school there where the music teacher had been an assistant to Ivor Atkins at Worcester Cathedral. In his teens, Joubert's schooling imbued him with a love of English cathedral music, over the years being influenced by the music of Elgar, Walton and Britten, as well as Bartók, Janacek, Stravinsky and Shostakovich. At the age of nineteen he won a scholarship to study at the Royal Academy of Music in London, where he gained a Royal Philharmonic Society prize. When he was twenty-four he married Mary, then teaching in a girls' secondary school in Hull, and wrote the ever-popular *Torches* carol for her pupils; in the same year, Barbirolli conducted the Hallé Orchestra in Joubert's *Overture* op 3 at the Cheltenham Festival.

Having lectured at both Hull and Birmingham Universities for many years, Joubert concentrates his time at his home in Moseley in composition, in 1997 completing his eighth opera *Jane Eyre*. The Birmingham Festival Choral Society commissioned him to compose a work to celebrate the Centenary of the City of Birmingham in 1989, and Jeremy Patterson conducted the premiere of *For the Beauty of the Earth* in Birmingham Cathedral on 25 November of that year, in the presence of the Lord Mayor and Lady Mayoress of Birmingham.

Since that date, BFCS has performed a number of Joubert's works, particularly in the 'Towards the Millennium' series of concerts. These include *Autumn Rain* (commissioned by Pamela Cook and Cantamus), *Blest Glorious Man* (commissioned by Nicholas Fisher for the Birmingham Bach Choir), and the second performance of *For the Beauty of the Earth*, conducted by Anthony Bradbury in 1995.

The choral symphony *For the Beauty of the Earth* makes a continuous whole formed of three movements without a break. The central movement for baritone solo is a setting of the poem 'God's Grandeur' by Gerard Manley Hopkins (1844-89). The texts for the outer movements come from the 1611 Authorised Version of the Bible, using Psalms 8 and 65, 148 and 104. During the final movement, Joubert quotes vv 1 and r from F S Pierpoint's hymn *For the Beauty of the Earth* to the tune 'Moseley' that he composed in 1965 for the publication *Hymns for Church and School*.

John Joubert is joint Patron with composer Elis Pehkonen of the Birmingham Festival Choral Society.

JP

JOHN RUTTER (b 1945)
PSALMFEST
for soprano & tenor, chorus & orchestra

1. *O be joyful in the Lord* (Psalm 100) (chorus)
2. *I will lift up mine eyes* (Psalm 121) (chorus and optional soloists)
3. *Praise the Lord, O my soul* (Psalm 146) (chorus)
4. *The Lord is my shepherd* (Psalm 23) (soprano, tenor and chorus)
5. *Cantate Domino* (Psalm 96) (unaccompanied chorus)
6. *The Lord is my light* (Psalm 27) (soprano, tenor and chorus)
7. *O clap your hands* (Psalm 47 vv 1-7) (chorus)
8. *O how amiable are Thy dwellings* (Psalm 84) (soprano & tenor duet)
9. *O praise the Lord of Heaven* (Psalm 148) (double chorus)

John Rutter was born in London in 1945 and received his first musical education as a chorister at Highgate School. He went on to study music at Clare College, Cambridge, where he wrote his first published compositions and conducted his first recording while still a student.

His career in composition has embraced both large and small-scale choral works, orchestral and instrumental pieces, a piano concerto, two children's operas, music for television, and specialist writing for such groups as the Philip Jones Brass Ensemble and the King's Singers. His most recent larger choral works, *Requiem* (1985), *Magnificat* (1990) and *Psalmfest* (1993) have been performed many times in Britain, North America, and a growing number of other countries. He is perhaps best known for his Christmas carols, several of which feature in the well known Carols for Choirs series which he edited with Sir David Willcocks.

The nine movements of *Psalmfest* were written over a period of twenty years and first performed on 8 June 1993 in Dallas, Texas. The texts are all taken from the Psalms. Some or all the movements can be presented on any given occasion, seven being given on the occasion of the competition in the version for tenor and soprano soloists, choir and a small orchestral ensemble with organ.

DG

CHRISTOPHER BROWN (b 1943)
INVOCATION, op 90
for soprano, alto, tenor & bass soli, chorus & organ

In choosing the texts for *Invocation* I wanted not only to celebrate the birth of Christ but also to reflect on its significance for our own time and for our own lives. In the multi-faceted world in which we live, where great beauty, optimism and goodness rub shoulders with the tragedies of war, famine, natural disaster and man's inhumanity to man, and where new discoveries in science raise all sorts of questions about our position in the Universe, there is perhaps a greater need than ever before for a spiritual dimension to our lives. Whether that spirituality is specifically Christian or whether it is inspired by other cultures, traditions and quests, the basic needs are similar: to create a better world in which we can live in greater harmony;

Christopher Brown's *Invocation*, here setting anonymous words.
(Copyright Christopher Brown © 1999; reproduced by
kind permission of Musography.)

tolerance and peace.

Musically the work is derived from the acronym BCAD, and these four notes give rise to almost all of the musical material. The mystery of the opening organ introduction soon gives way to an extended choral celebration of Christmas in which the traditional plainchant associated with the words *Hodie Christus natust est* features prominently A gently reflective setting of Alice Meynell's visionary words in her poem *Christ in the Universe* reminds us of our relative insignificance in the face of the immensity of God's Universe. The third and fifth sections set typically colourful texts by D H Lawrence, framing a movement in which solo voices reflect on our individual roles and responsibilities. The final part returns to the music of the opening, transforming the original plainchant and reminding us that Christ's birth offers an opportunity for greater love and peace in our world.

Invocation was written in 1999 for the New Cambridge Singers, who gave its first performance in January 2000.

CB

ALAN BULLARD (b 1947)
CANTATE GLORIA
for unaccompanied choir

This was commissioned for the 1999 Convention of British Choral Directors, and was first performed by the massed delegates, conducted by Bruce Pullan.

RICHARD BLACKFORD (b 1954)
CANTICLE OF THE BIRDS
(from MIRROR OF PERFECTION)
for tenor, chorus & orchestra

THE WINNER OF MANY AWARDS AND PRIZES, RICHARD BLACKFORD has achieved particular eminence in the worlds of stage, film and television. He has the rare ability to write music of significance in a highly approachable idiom. The 40-minute Cantata to words of St Francis, *Mirror of Perfection,* for soloists, chorus and orchestra, was broadcast in a BBC2 film, partly shot in Assisi, on Easter Day 1999.

This short, charming movement is for solo voice with children's choir, strings, horns and harp.

HO

Sir Richard Rodney Bennett (b 1936)
THE GLORY AND THE DREAM
for chorus & organ

In 1998 the New Cambridge Singers invited Richard Rodney Bennett to write a major work for choir and organ to celebrate the Millennium. At a time when new music has difficulty finding widespread popular appeal, the commissioning of new works for amateur and semi-professional musicians is a vitally important part in the bridge-building process between composers and audiences, but it can place a very heavy financial burden on the often limited resources of the commissioning body. Nevertheless, a composer such as Bennett, who time and again has proved himself adept at tailoring his music to the specific needs of both the occasion and the performers without compromising his own style was felt to be ideally suited to the sort of work we had in mind, and we determined to press ahead with the difficult process of raising sufficient funds.

The world's first e-commission?
It was a most fortunate moment of inspiration to try our luck with the Internet, and to post an invitation to other choirs around the world to share in the commission. To our delight and astonishment we were immediately bombarded with enquiries from all corners of the globe. An extended sifting period followed, but in the end we were able to finalise contracts with fifteen other choirs from as far afield as Australia, Canada, Iceland, the UK and the USA. This unique use of the Internet for global musical co-operation will, we hope, point the way towards a new style of commissioning in the future which can only be of benefit to all parties; composer and publisher get wider circulation, sales and royalties for the new piece, while the commissioners are able to reduce their costs, and get an extra dose of that all-important commodity – publicity! Perhaps most important of all, more organisations get the opportunity to be involved in the commissioning process, and thereby experience the thrill of being responsible for the creation of new music.

The music

When I received the composer's manuscript last March I knew immediately that we had struck gold in this innovative venture. Living with the piece for the past year and, more recently, rehearsing it with the choir, has only succeeded in boosting that initial impression. The composer has chosen to create an extended unbroken cantata from Wordsworth's Ode *Intimations of Immortality from recollections of early childhood* (omitting stanzas 7 and 8), and has shown magnificently his skill at producing imaginatively original music that is both practical and immediately engaging.

The four-movement structure is meticulously put together, with carefully defined ideas and motifs that bind and clarify the half hour span of the music. The opening (and longest) movement is a relatively straightforward ABA structure in which the outer sections mirror the lyrical, pastoral character of the words in long melodic lines over delicately patterned organ figuration. The central section has a more dance-like mood that gradually builds to a substantial climax. The second and third movements represent the slow movement and scherzo of the work, and in the latter the organ remains silent for extended periods of unaccompanied singing. The finale opens with a lengthy paean of praise to nature, before relaxing into reflective memories of the work's first two movements and a quietly serene epilogue.

The New Cambridge Singers were privileged to give the premiere on 3 March 2001, and eagerly await reports from around the world of the first performances being given by the other participating choirs.

CB

6. COMPLETE LIST
OF PROGRAMMES & ARTISTS

THE JUDGES OF THE MILLENNIUM CHORAL COMPETITION attended twelve competing concerts, complete details of which are given here. The Woodstock Music Society gave their concert twice, the judges attended the second presentation on Saturday 10 December 2000.

30 September 2000: School Hall, Eton College
The Broadheath Singers/Windsor Sinfonia/ Robert Tucker
soloists: Jennifer Higgins, m-s; Michael Pearce, bar
FREDERICK DELIUS: *Songs of Sunset*
EDGAR BAINTON: *Before Sunrise*

18 November 2000: St Joseph's Church, Highgate Hill, London N 19
Highgate Choral Society/New London Orchestra/Ronald Corp
Jane Watts, organ
soloists: Carolyn Foulkes, s; Joanna Gamble, m-s;
Andrew Murgatroyd, t; Edward Caswell bass
BENJAMIN DALE: *The Paling of the Stars*
BENJAMIN BRITTEN: *Cantata Academica*
SULLIVAN: *Te Deum Laudamus [Festival Te Deum]*

25 November 2000: St Cuthbert's Parish Church, Edinburgh
'A Centenary Celebration Concert'
The Savoyard Chorus and Orchestra/David Lyle
Martyn Strachan and John Kitchen, organ
soloists: Elizabeth McKeon, s; Heather Boyd, con;
Steven Griffin, t; Bruce Graham, bar
SULLIVAN: *Overture 'In Memoriam'*
SULLIVAN: *The Golden Legend*

9 and 10 December 2000: St Mary Magdalene Church, Woodstock
'Agincourt'
Woodstock Music Society/Paul Ingram
Speaker (in Walton): Philip Cade
ALAN BULLARD: *Cantate Gloria*
BRIDGE: *A Prayer*
WALTON: *Suite from Henry V*
ARNOLD: *Little Suite No 1*
DYSON: *Agincourt*

10 February 2001: Sheffield Cathedral
Sheffield Oratorio Chorus/Sheffield Cathedral Girl's Choir
South Yorkshire Symphony Orchestra/Alan Eost
Peter Heginbotham, organ; Katharine Napier, piano
soloists: Miranda McDonnell, s; Nick Sales, t;
David Townend, bar
FINZI: *Lo! The Full, Final Sacrifice* (for choir and organ)
LE FLEMING: *Five Psalms*
VAUGHAN WILLIAMS: *Pilgrim's Journey*

3 March 2001: St John's College Chapel, Cambridge
'The Glory and the Dream'
New Cambridge Singers/Christopher Brown
Peter Barley, organ
soloists: Joanna Miles, s; Madeleine Holmes, s;
Katy Edgcombe, con; Jane Richardson, con;
George Smerdon, t; David Gadd, t; David Sheppard, t;
Charles Jones, bass; Tim Atkinson, bass
SIR LENNOX BERKELEY: *Festival Anthem*
SIR RICHARD RODNEY BENNETT: *The Glory and the Dream*
CHRISTOPHER BROWN: *Invocation*
BRITTEN: *Rejoice in the Lamb*

17 March 2001: The Cathedral, Bury St Edmunds
'Concert of British Music'
St Edmundsbury Bach Choir and Orchestra/
St Cecilia Singers/Harrison Oxley
Michael Bawtree, organ and harpsichord
soloist: Gordon Pullin, t
HANDEL: *Zadok the Priest*
RUBBRA: *Song of the Soul*
STANFORD: *Ave Atque Vale*
RICHARD BLACKFORD: *Canticle of the Birds*
ELGAR: Overture *Cockaigne*
GEORGE OLDROYD: *Jhesu Christ, Saint Mary's Sone*
PARRY: *Blest Pair of Sirens*

24 March 2001: Hereford Cathedral
Dr Roy Massey Retirement Concert
Hereford Choral Society/Orchestra da Camera/Roy Massey
soloists: Julie Kennard, s; Robert Johnston, t
FINZI: *Intimations of Immortality*
ELGAR: *Serenade for Strings*
PARRY: *Ode on the Nativity*

24 March 2001: Guildford Cathedral
'This Sceptr'd Isle'
Guildford Choral Society/BBC Concert Orchestra/
Hilary Davan Wetton
David Gibson, organ
soloist: Christine Rice, m-s
DYSON: *Agincourt*
ELGAR: *Sea Pictures*
PARRY: *The Chivalry of the Sea*
ELGAR: *The Music Makers*

31 March 2001: Birmingham Cathedral
'A Concert of Birmingham "Firsts"'
Birmingham Festival Choral Society/Boys of St Chad's Cathedral Choir/
Birmingham Festival Choral Society Orchestra/David Saint (organ)/
Anthony Bradbury and Jeremy Patterson
soloists: Constance Novis, s; Hyacinth Nicholls, m-s;
Mark Wilde, t; Alan Fairs, b-bar
D'ERLANGER: *Messe de Requiem*
JOUBERT: Choral Symphony *For the Beauty of the Earth*

31 March 2001: St Anselm's Church, Belmont
Stanmore Choral Society/Chandos Chamber Orchestra/
David Gould
Nicholas Shaw, organ
soloists: Rosalind Waters, s; Christopher Hogan, t;
Julian Stocker, t; Stephen Alder, b;
WILLIAM LLOYD WEBBER: *The Divine Compassion*
RUTTER: *Psalmfest*

22 April 2001: Milton Keynes Theatre
'A Space Odyssey'
The Milton Keynes Chorale/Milton Keynes City Orchestra/John Gibbons
Tim Grant-Jones, organ
soloist: Jeremy Huw Williams, bar
HOLST: *Mars* [*The Planets*]
JOUBERT: Choral Symphony *The Choir Invisible*
STRAUSS: *Also sprach Zarathustra* [opening]
W G WHITTAKER: *The Cœlestial Spheare*
HOLST: *Jupiter* [*The Planets*]
VAUGHAN WILLIAMS: *Toward the Unknown Region*

7. THE COMPETING CHOIRS:
the singing members

AS FAR AS IT HAS BEEN POSSIBLE TO CHECK THE FOLLOWING ARE THE members of the choirs who competed in the Millennium Choral Competition. The choirs are listed in alphabetical order.

BROADHEATH SINGERS
Sopranos: Ann Beauchamp Katie Beauchamp Betty Brown Sandy Clare Marguerite Crockett Betty Davis Angela Dickson Vicky Hartley Margaret Hawthorn Sheila Johnson Siobhan Ladyman Julia Lewis Gay Livingston Maureen Lloyd-Jones Maureen Kyte Joan McBirney Margaret Malindine Jill Mans Grace Pullinger Mary Rosso Hazel Staddon Jan Story Avice Turner Margaret Wilkins

Altos: Pat Barnett Flick Caisley Margaret Carloa Barbara Clark Hannah Dunmow Jean Gershon Dorothy Godfrey Helen Harris Val Jeffries Pat Johnson Paddy O'Brien John Overton Pat Parker Julie Parsons Ruth Sanford Angela Schiller Pamela Shepherd Heather Skinner Jennifer Steele Janet Trousdale Alison Tucker Vanessa Watkins Christine Webb Joyce Wolff

Tenors: Ian Brentnall Colin Bromelow Nicholas Brown Jackie Clarke Andrew Johnson Peter King David Miller Edward Rabbitt John Turner David Wade

Basses: Lewis Beddison Keith Bramich Douglas Dickson Peter Griffiths Leslie Grout Fred Hartley Graham Jones Roger Lyon Douglas Rust John Salmon David Tilley Martin Warren Christopher Whitehouse Charles Wolff

BIRMINGHAM FESTIVAL CHORAL SOCIETY
BOYS OF ST CHAD'S CATHEDRAL CHOIR
(Director: Richard Longman)
Andrew Long (Head Chorister) Harry Ager Christopher Clinton Luke Connolly Dano Genockey Joseph Holt Chad Kennedy Andrew Martin Andrew Moxley Thomas O'Carroll Thomas Stephenson Simon Stilwell John Thome Yury Villalonga-Stanton

BIRMINGHAM FESTIVAL CHORAL SOCIETY
First Sopranos: Kate Adams Jackie Amatya Jenni Bradbury Kathy Carter Tessa Farrell Esther Henley Janice Hobday Christine Powell Anne Quirk

Elissa Renouf Evelyn Smylie Susanna Spall Janet Vosper Helen Walker
Helena Wiezel

Second Sopranos: Margaret Allen Jill Bevan Julia Brooks Katherine Campbell-Legg Lucy Cole Sylvie Dattas Susan Eceleston Sue Ingleby Olga Jackson
Margaret Knowles Mary McEvoy Lizzy Rankin Helen Rouse Pat Sack
Marilyn Seeckts Norma Southwick Marianne Watson Cath Whatcott Michele
White Sheila Whitehouse

First Altos: Jean Bacon June Bacon Janet Brookes Liz Collins Nan Haigh
Jenny Harvey Katherine Holwill Judith Hughes Therese Ingleby Margaret
Jones Theresa Kavanagh Melanie King Kaili Clenon Chris Pascal Margund
Rowe Hazel Smith Rosemary Watkins Angela Willis Ellen Whitehouse Jill
Wood Marrian Yates

Second Altos: Carole Atkinson Elizabeth Black Sarah Black Tricia Bradbury
Jean Caswell Sally Darby Shirley Evans Sarah Gordon Kath Hawker Caroline
Liberson Lindsay Martin Sheila Moore Hilary Morgan Gill Newman Ann
Pitt Julia Sinirns Sue Todd Louise Vivian Sara White

First Tenors: Michael Alder Pelham Barton Linda Batten David Fletcher
Alan Guest Robin Moore Peter Regan

Second Tenors: James Dowden Ron Guest David Jones Chris Kent Philip
Quirk Paul O'Dell Bob Skeicher Dominic Smith

First Basses: Derek Bevan Tom Brown Julian Edwards Andrew Guymer
Richard Kaye Nick Lampert Tim Law Roger Monk Keith Rowe

Second Basses: Gordon Allen Peter Asquiffi James Bradbury Fred Hathway
Barry Lankester Eric Rickeffs Robert Warren

GUILDFORD CHORAL SOCIETY

First Sopranos: Kate Andrews Caroline Colmer Lyn Daniels Sheila Emerton
Janee Foxon Jane Fulcher Patricia Kawar Kathryn Knox Lucy Massy Diana
Medlicott Felicia Pheasant Sarah Phillpot Josie Pitchforth Claire Pocock
Clare Thornton-Wood Dorien van de Belt Hanneke van't Veer Catherine
Watmore Annabel Wilson Mandi Robinson Janet Yendole

Second Sopranos: Margaret Barrett Shirley Barrett Marian Coom Diane
Cuff Gina Dando Sara Davies Nicola Fournel Martha Golden Jackie
Hagan Kathleen Hall Elizabeth Hedges Lucy Jackson Christina Lawson
Sue Lister Denise Lynch Gaynor Malin Zoe Norris-Hill Joan Pratley Liz

Scott Ann Sheard Claire Sheather Susan Smith Isobel Squire Natalie Thurley Jane Tingley Belinda Usmar Celia Vaile Gillian Williams Celia Woodward Julia Macfarlane Suzanne Goacher

First Altos: Siobhan Carroll Fiona Collett Beryl Disley Valerie Dixon Henry Liz Healey Maureen Hellyer Silke Helseler Rowena Hill Jeannie Hodkin Deb Hounsell Ros Hurst Ruth Jorden Mary Korndorffer Ulreke Lentz Denise Lunn Amelia Lyon Pam Mattos Stella May Claire McCreery Robin Pass Cynthia Plewman Lesley Pratt Tina Procter Julie Rickard Sheila Rowell Caroline Sawers Barbara Stokes Caroline Turnbull Penny Van Eupen Yee Lui Williams Gill Wood Ann Woodriff Laura Claridge Henrietta Bradshaw Karen Faulkner

Second Altos: Angela Bushnell Carole Cameron Jane Cork Sally Critchlow Dorothy Downer Janet Epton Kate Fisher Bridget Flett Marilyn Mercer Meg Moore Beryl Northam Sarah Rogers Cherry Sheppard Alison Stainsbury Catherine Wands Joyce Woodbridge Sue Woolard-White

First Tenors: John Mayle Geoffrey Quick Guy Vogel Michael Wheatley Mark White

Second Tenors: Nigel Bain Chris Chester Geoff Disley Andy Gill Mike Hall Gavin Pass Bryan Yendole

First Basses: David Greenwood Keith Malin Anthony May Huw Michael Felix Plazza Dennis Rowe Michael Smith Keith Torbet John Trimming Mark Ward-Jackson John Winterton Hugh Ralph

Second Basses: Tom Barnard Roger Buck Ralph Carver Greg Casbolt Trevor Davies Ken Elsom Nigel Garbutt Michael Herzig John Jones Barry Norman Edward Pepper John Turnbull Don Watson Stephen Wright

HEREFORD CHORAL SOCIETY
First Sopranos: Elizabeth Allen Sophie Allen Jane Ayres Lynne Bradley Trudy Brookes Rosamund Bumbam Annette Carter Elizabeth Cripwell Gill Curtis Christine Escott Fiona Field Doreen Foster Maria Foxton Barbara Gibson Jenny Hancock Lucy Hargrove Gillian Hodges Philornena Kearne Diane Leng Sarah Logan Elizabeth Miller Kate Price Elizabeth Rimmer Barbara Shore Hilary Smallwood Hazel Smith Anne Smyth Angela Speight Barbara Thomas Edith Tout Gillian Walde Pamela White Terri Wilkins

Second Sopranos: Barbara Atkins Maureen Bemand Margaret Bentley-Leek

Gillian Bland   Gillian Brimacombe   Julie Bunker   Margaret Castle   Valerie
Cornwall Christine Dennington Barbara Dutton Pamela Emes Linda Farr
Susan Furnival Wendy Hart Anne Hyde-Smith Julia Kilvert Lynne Lloyd
Cessa Moore   Pat Oliver   Brenda Preece   Anne Rodger

First Altos: Jill Bowen   Jenny Bradley   Sue Brambell   Celia Brown   Hilary
Bulmer Kath Card Margaret Chappell Lesley Conning Val Culley Vera
Dale Jean Davies Tricia Davies Catherine Evans Sebastian Field Liz Gates
Carola Girling Jenny Grant Mildred Gray Ann Griffiths Penny Hall Margaret
Helps Lizza Henderson Beryl Jackson Helen Jackson Kate Jones Rachel
Lewis Maggie Love Christine Mackay Margaret Neal Meriel Oliver Sue
Plant Tibb Richardson Olwen Roberts Frances Roper Anna Teresa Rossini
Jo Swindells Margaret Taylor Sally Wilmott Barbara Young

Second Altos: Linda Arnold Elizabeth Bennett Julia Birley Jill Boyd Jennifer
Budd Anne Bull Sandra Devenish Diana Dewé Kitty Glennie-Smith Kate
Greenall Marian Hale Eleanor James Dorrie Leng Margaret Lowther Anne
Oldroyd Dora Parry Benda Plears Barbara Pilkington Pauline Powell Wendy
Previté Brenda Smith Kay Taylor Janet Wardle Christine Wheatley Susan
Whitaker Elizabeth Wreford

First Tenors: Alex Draper Tony Giles Robert Milan Chris Robins Aneu-
rin Thomas Andrew Wheatley Robert Wreford

Second Tenors: Richard Birt Nick Bulmer Philip Havelock Tony
Hollingworth Frank Johnson Tony Malpas Peter Williams

First Basses: Jim Birley Ray Boddington John Dutton Paul Hemmings
Raymond Highley Ray Morgan Glyn Morris John Newton Roger Norman
Robert Parry David Plowman George Richardson Bill Smyth E William
Taylor Peter Tomlinson lain Watt

Second Basses: Hal Baptist Neil Brambell Richard Bull John Ellis Richard
Henderson James Latham Chris Mackay Donald Preece Guy Rawlinson
Alan Taylor Howard Tomlinson

HIGHGATE CHORAL SOCIETY
First Sopranos: Vicki Ambery Jane Blundell   Gloria Comer Jude Evans
Norah Foss Pat Fraser Carol George Helena Goldie Lucy Hammersley
Vicky Lennon Helena Lezard Sue Lucas-Stone Sarah McLachlan Helen
Mignano Andrea Morris Verity Sherwood Sally Sinclair-Webb Thelma
Tennant Marion Thomas Carol Watts Geraldine Willford Hilary Wilmer

Second Sopranos: Di Arthur Paula Attree Helen Bantock Jackie Benson Sue Blake Anne Boutwood Pat Chadwick Pat Dale Ros Dixon Chris Driver Esther Dunsone Julia Edwards Catherine Fried Angela Hughes Ursula Owen Dilys Oliphant Carolyn Pascall Kirsten Pollock Deborah Schneebeli-Morell Margaret Scammell Molly Scopes Lalage Stephens Martha Tyrone Alison Watson Jenny Weston

First Altos: Marcia Beer Anne Bouvier Noreen Branson Catherine Budgett-Meakin Ruth Chadwick Joyce Coomber Glenda Cornwell Marion Donaldson Elisabeth Flintspach Fiona Hackett Miranda Halsby Jane Jackling Anne Johnson Rosemary Lewin Jocelyn Lucas Angela Mendis Ann Middleton Val Nield Pat Painter Maggie Pringle Isabel Raphael Sonja Roston Barbara Segal Shirley Shelton

Second Altos: Sheila Evered Helene Gordon Cicely Hopper Naomi Lobbenberg Kathryn Metzenthin Joy Newman Joan Pegram Yvonne Robinson Katharin Schopflin Elaine Spicer Heidi Walkden Lydia Weston Jennifer Winn Ailie Worster

Tenors: Ken Alberman Malcolm Crow Alan Davis Andrew Frankl George Gretton Chris Moore Wil Newcomb Roger Scopes Henning Sieverts Don Skinner

First Basses: Chris Ashley Geoff Comer John Denza Brian Hardisty Peter Hildrew Geoffrey Hughes Tim Shelton

Second Basses: Nick Balaam Roger Dean Paul Filmer John Hammond Simon Harrison Christopher Johnson Andrew Moor Huw Organ Ashitey Ollennu Dieter Pevsner Martin Upham Andrew Urquhart David Waterhouse Philip Weston Jeffrey Young

THE MILTON KEYNES CHORALE
Sopranos: Nicola Adshead Rosemary Blackwell Pat Brook Margaret Brown Lisa Burns Margaret Caen Elisabeth Clarke Mariana Cooke Linda Coveney Jenny Daish Sue Davies Christine Dickens Daphne Fawcett Krystyna Foster Ryoko Haga Felicity Head Fran Herety Sheila Hobkinson Jean Hulley Atsuko Ishitoya Norma Jamieson Alison Kerr Anne Kershaw Marilyn Long Ruth Martin Ruth Meardon Mary Mullett Hilary O'Donoghue Carole Probert Jean Reed Andrea Rees Anne Robinson Marlene Robinson Jacquie Rogers Judy Rose Milena Seckarova Jo Sheppard Gi Sierant Janet Spencer Joyce Taylor Deborah Ward Jacqui Watson Janet Williams Rhiannon Wilson-Price

Altos: Margaret Ashton Liz Baatz Gillian Bartram Glenys Bloomfield Jane Canvin Sue Daish Lona Davies Siobhan Duff Caroline Eyley Clare Francis Mary Golcher Teresa Hadley Sharon Harris Vivienne Holliday Sally Jones Sylvia Laybourn Jenny Lee Anne MacKenzie Barbara Middleton Laura Mundell Jessamine Onslow Rebecca Pasha Mary Pawley Lesley Pyke Bridget Queiros Janet Rees Marjorie Reilly Rhona Sayer Shirley Scrutton Jenni Smith Sue Smith Deb Spinks Rowena Taylor Marilyn Thomas Aniko Vertesy Gill Vincent Meg Vischer Joyce Whiffen Sally Wilson Jane Wolfson Penny Yates

Tenors: Patrick Bligh Vic Brennan John Burgess Vic Canty Don Head Tony Izod Geoff Lamperd Robert Meardon Nick Fisher Charles Francis David Parris Roger Pearce David Pye Magnus Ramage Tony Robson David Scutton James Wharton

Basses: Brian Coulstock Ray Dines Derek Franklin Jim Gibson John Hancock Robin Haseldine Malcolm Hayes Ray Merrington Clive Morris Stephen Morris Peter Osborne Bill Prescott Peter Priestley Martin Rayner Tony Seward Sam Snook George Tapner Alan Thomas Eddie Thompson John Wheaver Trevor Winters

NEW CAMBRIDGE SINGERS
Sopranos: Audrey Dean   Judith Hall   Philippa Harris Claire Hoople Madeleme Holmes   Joanna Miles   Carrie Pemberton   Lydia Smaliwood Amanda Williams

Altos: Maggie Copestake Katy Edgcombe Friedericke Jeans Claire Parker Jane Richardson Allison Toogood Angela Watts Rachel Wroth

Tenors: Michael Antcliff David Gadd David Sheppard George Smerdon Stephen Toogood

Basses: Tim Atkinson Charles Beresford Martin Gent Charles Jones Jeremy Pemberton Richard Prince Alan Rickard Phil Ridley

ST EDMUNDSBURY BACH CHOIR
ST CECILIA SINGERS
Hannah Barham   Elizabeth Cockerton   Elizabeth Davies Tanya Kewell Hayley Last Siobhan Leeks Victoria Leeks Clare-Alice Maynard Charlotte Roberts Naomi Rogers Esther Rutter Alana Self Kerensa Slade Stephanie Vicat Nikki Werker

ST EDMUNDSBURY BACH CHOIR

Sopranos: Eileen Adams Helen Benckendorff Betty Birkby Geraldine Birt Anne Bloomfield Ann Brown Janet Brown Marguerite Budden Penelope Carter Joanna Caruth Jan Chandler Frances Cox Coral Cummings Linda Downing Mary Elliott Ruth Foreman Jean Hartley Celia Jeal Caroline King Ruth Lee Kate Leigh Irene Millard Eileen Morris Christina Newns Jean Pearson Jill Reynolds-Law Lucy Rickard Josephine Roberts Pam Robinson Judy Rolfe Jenny Schram Hilary Scott Jennifer Swallow Glen Taylor Sylvia Taylor Betty Thompson Jane Turnbull Jill Van-de-Plasse Mari-Louise Waghorn Carmel Walker Annabel Whitter Sue Willcox

Altos: Meriden Askem Ricky Balaam Margaret Bellamy Miriam Black Elizabeth Bollworthy Joy Bolwell Jo Burrell Anne Bustin Sue Carling Brenda Cerhan Jan Clark Joan Clarke Ann Curtis Ann Daniels Lynne Darling Ann Dyball Jill Dyer Shiela Evans Hilary Griffiths David Hartley Liz Hartley Ruth Haward Carolyn Heywood Elizabeth Hollingsworth Margaret Holt Janet Keeble Caroline Kewell Anne Kilner Janet King Ruth Lister Sarah Lord Beryl Lucas Margaret Messenger Rose Ornbo Mary-Clare O'Sullivan Judith Peacock Georgina Pharaoh Audrey Rogers Muriel Rogers Sarah Roper Claire Rose Nikki Rycroft Jean Taylor Sue Thompson Madeline Tildsley Hilary Voysey Sally Watson Joyce Withers Marjorie Wolf Jane Wright

Tenors: Ralph Baldwin John Brown Christopher Burch Phil Clennell David Fosbuary Frank Gash Martin Hadley-Brown Peter Helliwell Stephen Roberts John Wheeldon

Basses: George Agnew Geoffrey Birkby Christopher Boothby Paul Caldwell David Dean David Ellwood Bob Emery David Evans Dick Evans Keith Everett Frank Flynn Keith Foreman David Hance David Harrison Mike Heywood Ralph Hughes-Lewis James Knowles David Lord Bob Morris Colin Ratcliffe Peter Rose John Slade Alec Strahan Mike Voysey Peter Wallin David Ward Peter Whitlock

THE SAVOYARD CHORUS

Sopranos: Hilary Anderson Adrienne Burgess Heather Coates Margaret Cormack Shirley Glynn Elizabeth Harry Ann Heavens Caroline Kerr Linny Lawson Norma Macdonald Sheila Mackintosh Fiona Main Seonaid Martin Pat McKerrow Joyce Murray Anna Newton Ann O'Reagan Mary Scott Liz Thomson

Altos: Katharine Barbour Joyce Boyd Wendy Crawford Kate Duffield

Catherine Harkin Liz Landsman Carol Macbeth Evelyn McHolland Marion Ramsay Ann Scott-Fleming Susan Sheppard Pat Slugocki Jane Smart Irene Vernon Alison York Micky York

Tenors: Andrew Brown Brian Caddow Stewart Coghill Neil French Alan Hogg Ian Lawson George McHollan George Rae Peter Scott

Basses: George Burgess Gordon Campbell John Howden Gareth Jacobs Craig Macbeth Ross Main William Parry Harry Payne Craig Robertson Ken Robinson George Wilson Robin Wilson Rolly York

SHEFFIELD ORATORIO CHOIR
Sopranos: Gillian Bell Ruth Crowley Pamela Durling Julia Fryer Marie Hebden Susan Lack Suzanne Mason Lois McGrath Margaret Millington Kathryn Sanders Janet Saunders Patricia Schofield Eileen Selvey Mary Seneviratne Margaret Thompson June Thompson-Graham Elisabeth Vallance Meriel Watson Ros Witten

Altos: Zdenka Adamova Carol Atherton Alsion Ballington Jane Barwell Michelle Bullivant Diana Bowns Shirley Brumby Sarah Cooper Elsie Eland Hazel Elliott-Kemp Averil Fleetwood Pauline Garratt Clare Griffiths Margaret Hawksworth Barbara Hawley Christine Hemsley Pamela Horn Kaye Horsfield Philippa Hughes Kathy Lamb Catherine Morris Clare Power Amanda Simpson Kathryn Swift Claire Woodhead Eyrl Wyn-Jones Janet Young

Tenors: John Abbott Andy Bolton Bill Clarke Laurence Coates Geoffrey Edwards David Oakley David Price Geoff Ridsdale Chris Saunders

Basses: Roger Atkin Keith Barstow Paul Chaplais Robin Edwards   Ralph Hebden Philip Hirst Andrew Horn Paul Jordan Roger Ledbetter Gordon Matthewman Daniel Power John Shaw Dave Webber Peter Webster

STANMORE CHORAL SOCIETY
Sopranos: Margaret Allman Daniela Amasanti Pat Bowden Frances Bradford Sylvia Cope Kath Earls Marion Easton Marilyn Finester Pauline Forsyth Maggy Gardner Janette Goss Mary Haines Marian Holding Pauline Jackson Daphne Johnson Magdalena Pletsch Jean Rainbow Pamela Rance Margaret Reid Pauline Seaton June-Ann Storey Win Walmsley Barbara Whitten Kathryn Wolfendale

Altos: Sheila Birch Margaret Blake Barry Bright Elizabeth Clarke Wendy

Davis Maureen Drew Frances Goldingay Nina Grimwood Pam Haines Jill Henshaw Malou Heyman Hilary Hibbert Sandra Imrie Elise Longman Jana Markham Hilary Marsden Beth Morris Bernadette O'Gorman Rilla Paterson Gill Wells Jane Williams

Tenors: Ken Bowden Edmund Butterworth Glyn Marchant Irene Pyke John Watson

Basses: George Arch Bill Brooks Tony Dutton Gerry Earls Patrick Forsyth Bill Gibson Bernard Heyman John Jones John Longbons Mike Longman Brian Seaton Roger Smithies Reginald Somes Henry Watson

WOODSTOCK MUSIC SOCIETY CHOIR

Sopranos: Anne Askwith Tricia Astley Elizabeth Bloomfield Margaret Bulleyment Adrienne Evans Teresa Finlay Celia Garrick Lindsay Hague Annie Hawes Evelyn Hendy Nancy Kiley Lucy Martin Liz Mills Anita Mutton Hanny Nicholson Mary Phipps Rosalyn Roulston Helen Saunders-Gill Jane Scott Liz Seddon Mary Small Susie Tomlin Sue Townsend Barbara Vaughan Helen Woolley

Altos: Wilma Anderson Miriam Burton Jennifer Candy Amanda Drake-Brockman Cordie Edwards Kathryn Ellis Falmai Gathercole Jessica Knott Elspeth Lewis Shirley Linfield Joyce Morris Liz Newton Ann Parsons Val Phillips Gilliane Sills Hazel Smith Rachel Strachan Sue Tee Sally Vaux Jo Waddams Bettye Ward Sarah-Jane Ward Jane Webber Mary Weston Jane Wood Jennie Woolridge June Wright

Tenors: Robin Alden John Banbury Will Clark Michael Collard Mike Deacon John Garrick Roger Mason David Muston Keith Oxtoby David Phipps

Basses: Phil Bloomfield Brian Carlick Jimmy Clifton Geoff Hirst Patrick Irwin David Machin Roderick Nicholson Bob Ritchie Stuart Seager Richard Sills Antony Smith Mike Smith Elvet Thomas Colin Townsend Rhys Williams.

8. SOURCES OF WORKS PERFORMED

AS WE HAVE ALREADY SEEN, SOURCING THE PERFORMING materials for many of the works considered in the competition was not always as straightforward as the promoters might have wished. This is to document the publisher or other sources where the vocal scores, orchestral scores and sets of orchestral parts were found and from where they might be obtained by future performers. Those marked * are out of copyright, + signifies the vocal score is in print. 'Chorus' means SATB choir unless otherwise stated. Several choirs found they could make considerable financial savings by borrowing public or other library sets of the vocal scores.

Bainton: Before Sunrise (20'15" + 13'48" + 8'23" + 17'09" = 59'35")
for contralto or mezzo-soprano, chorus & orchestra (note the first movement is for orchestra alone) (3+1 2+1 2+1 3+1 4331 timp perc 2hp str)
Score and parts: Stainer & Bell

Richard Rodney Bennett: The Glory and the Dream +
(11'29" + 4'56" + 6'32" + 7'47" = 30'34")
for chorus & organ
Vocal score: J & W Chester (Music Sales)

Berkeley: Festival Anthem (12' 20")
for soprano & tenor soli, chorus & organ
Vocal score: J & W Chester (Music Sales)

Blackford: Canticle of the Birds + (5'22")
for tenor solo, childrens choir, horn, harp, strings
[from *Mirror of Perfection* for soprano, baritone, chorus, childrens choir and orchestra (3 horns, harp, perc, strings)
Score and parts: London Music, 44 Parliament Hill, London NW3 2TN.]
See Internet: www.blackford.co.uk

Bridge: A Prayer (18' 10")
for chorus & orchestra
Score and parts: Stainer & Bell (2(1)222 4331 timp perc strings)
The Frank Bridge Trust has a loan set of vocal scores available at no charge.

Britten: Cantata Academica + (21' 20")
for soprano, alto, tenor and bass soli, chorus & orchestra
(2(1)222 4231 timp perc 2hp pf bells str)
Score and parts: Boosey & Hawkes

Britten: Rejoice in the Lamb, Op 30 + (18' 30")
for treble, alto, tenor & bass soli, chorus and organ
(also orch Imogen Holst: 1111 1000 perc org str)
Score and parts: Boosey & Hawkes

Christopher Brown: Invocation, Op 90 + (25' 45")
for SATB obligati, double chorus & organ
Vocal score: Musography, 6 Station Road, Catworth, Cambs OE18 0PE

Alan Bullard: Cantate Gloria + (1' 50")
Chorus a capella
Vocal score: Cathedral Music

Dale: Before the Paling of the Stars (15'53")
for chorus & orchestra (2132 3000 timp perc cel hp strings)
Scores and parts: Boosey & Hawkes

Delius: Songs of Sunset + (30'30")
soprano, baritone, chorus & orchestra (3334 4231 timp perc hp celesta strings)
Score and parts: Universal
The Broadheath Singers obtain vocal scores from Hillingdon and
Nottingham, Public Libraries

Dyson: Agincourt (24'59")
chorus & orchestra (2222 4331 timp perc hp strings)
Score and parts: Novello (Music Sales)

Elgar: The Music Makers + (37'36")
mezzo-soprano, chorus & orchestra(3333 4331 timp perc hp strings)
Score and parts: Novello (Music Sales)

d'Erlanger: Messe de Requiem
(4'10" + 4'14" + 2'00" + 12'17" + 7'27" + 5'06" + 7'49" + 6'12" + 10'38" = 59'53")
for soprano, mezzo-soprano, tenor and bass, chorus, organ (*ad lib*) & orchestra. No longer available from its original publisher (Schott). Complete
performing materials (3(1)222 4331 timp perc bells hp org strings) were
written specially for BFCS's performance and are available from BFCS; full
score and orchestral parts also held by Lewis Foreman.

Finzi: Lo! the Full, Final Sacrifice (1945)+ (14')
for chorus and organ (orchestral version 2222 4231 timp perc hp org str)
Score and parts: Boosey & Hawkes

Finzi: Intimations of Immortality (43')+
for tenor, chorus and orchestra
(3(1) 2+1 2+1 2+1 4331 timp perc hp strings)
Score and parts: Boosey & Hawkes

Joubert: The Choir Invisible (31' 25")
for baritone, chorus & orchestra (3+1 333 4331 timp perc pf hp org strings)
Score and parts: Novello (Music Sales)

Joubert: For the Beauty of the Earth (36' 50")
for baritone, chorus & orchestra (3+1 333 4331 timp perc pf hp org str)
Score and parts: Novello (Music Sales)
Birmingham Public Library has a set of vocal scores.

Le Fleming: Five Psalms (36'52")
for soprano, chorus & orch (2222+1 4330 hp timp perc str)
Score and parts: J & W Chester (Music Sales)

Lloyd Webber: Divine Compassion (Parts I & II: ca 40')
for soprano, two tenors and bass, chorus and organ.
Vocal scores were specially printed for this performance and the performance
set are available for hire from the Stanmore Choral Society.

Oldroyd: Jhesu Christ, St Mary's Sone (26'05")
for tenor, chorus & orchestra (2322 2200 timp perc harpsichord hp strings)
Score and parts: Novello (Music Sales)

Parry: Blest Pair of Sirens +(10'44")
for double choir & orchestra (2223 4331 timp org strings)
Score and parts: Novello (Music Sales)
Vocal scores were borrowed from Suffolk County Library

Parry: The Chivalry of the Sea *(14'14")
for chorus (SSATB) & orchestra (3333 4231 timp perc hp org strings)
Score and parts: Although published by Novello they can no longer supply
this work; performing materials are privately held (enquiries via BMS).

Parry: Ode on the Nativity (25' 15")
for soprano, chorus & orchestra
(2333 4231 timp hp org str)
Scores and parts: Novello (Music Sales)

Rubbra: Song of the Soul (11'18") +
for chorus (SSATBB) & orchestra (hp timp strings)
Score and parts: Lengnick (music Sales)

John Rutter: Psalmfest (45') +
for soprano, tenor, chorus & orchestra
(2(1) 222 4331 timp glock xyl perc hp strings)
Score and parts: Oxford University Press

Stanford: Ave Atque Vale* (18'00")
for chorus and orchestra (222+1 2+1 4331 timp perc hp org strings)
Score and parts: Stainer & Bell
Some vocal scores were provided by Glasgow Cathedral Choir

Sullivan: Te Deum Laudamus (Festival Te Deum) * + (32' 48")
for soprano & orchestra with *ad lib* brass band
(2(1)222+1 4231 (+ brass band/ensemble *ad lib*) timp org strings)
Score and parts: Novello (Music Sales)
Note: this work is also available from R Clyde, 6 Whitelands Ave,
Chorleywood Herts WD3 5RD, who has vocal scores for sale.

Sullivan: The Golden Legend* +
(9' + 11'30" + 23'46" + 18' + 8'07" + 5'48" + 9'20" + 6' = 91'31")
for soprano (Elsie), alto (Ursula), tenor (Prince Henry), baritone (Lucifer),
baritone (Forester - can double with Lucifer), chorus, organ and orchestra
(3333 4331 timp perc hp org strings)
Score and parts: Novello (Music Sales)
Note: this work is also available from R Clyde, 6 Whitelands Ave,
Chorleywood Herts WD3 5RD, who has vocal and full scores for sale.

Vaughan Williams: Toward the Unknown Region + (12' 11")
for chorus and orchestra (32+1 2+1 2 4331 timp 2hp org str)
Score and parts: Stainer & Bell
Many public libraries hold sets of vocal scores of this work.

Vaughan Williams: Pilgrim's Journey: a cantata (40')

for soprano, tenor and baritone, chorus and orchestra
(2(1) 2(1) 22 4231 perc glock xyl harp (or piano) strings)
various reductions possible including that used at Sheffield: flute, trumpet, piano, organ, percussion and strings.
Score and parts: Oxford University Press

W G Whittaker: The Cœlestial Spheare (12'05")

for chorus and orchestra (2 1+1 23 4331 timp perc strings)
Formerly published in vocal score by Oxford University Press;
performing materials were obtained from the Scottish Music
Information Centre in Glasgow.

9. CHORAL WORKS BY BRITISH COMPOSERS
researching the repertoire

A WIDE-RANGING REPERTOIRE LIST WAS CIRCULATED TO THOSE considering entering the Millennium Choral Competition. Its function was not prescriptive but to suggest works and composers worth exploring. This is reproduced here. Those works from the list which were actually played are not revisited here but are listed in section 8.

Sir Granville Bantock

There are two extended works by Bantock and a number of shorter ones. Of these *The Song of Songs* runs for some 2 hours, but has the advantage that in the past extracts have been viable in their own right. The complete score, which is arranged in five extended movements, requires six soloists, chorus and large orchestra; several of the movements can be performed separately, as could the choruses, and extracts running between 25 and 60 minutes, with or without soloists, would be viable and arresting (formerly Swan now Weinberger). Bantock's most celebrated work is probably *Omar Khayyam*. The BBC broadcast the complete work in 1979, timed at: Part 1 94 minutes; Part II 41 minutes; Part III 38 minutes. Parts I or III would make viable presentations in their own right (Mezzo-sop, tenor, baritone, chorus, orchestra). (Published by Breitkopf und Härtel; performing materials at BBC, enquiries via BMS)

Hubert Bath

The Legend of Nerbuddah: dramatic cantata
SSABarB soli, chorus and orchestra (Boosey & Hawkes) 24 min

Sir Arnold Bax

Bax wrote some half dozen choral works. Three are available on a Chandos CD. All are worth revival. The following (all Chappell) are not on CD: *The Morning Watch* Chorus and orchestra 19 mm; *St Patrick's Breastplate* Chorus and orchestra 16 minutes; *To the name Above Every Name* Soprano solo, chorus and orchestra 21 minutes

Sir Lennox Berkeley

There are a number of very effective choral works from Berkeley's maturity. His short oratorio *Jonah* was withdrawn after the first performance in 1937, but a revival in 1992 with organ suggests it would find a ready audience today. Tenor and baritone, chorus and orchestra (via BMS) 70 minutes.

Sir Arthur Bliss

Bliss's choral music (all Novello) is dominated by the Pastoral and Morning Heroes both programmed by choral societies from time to time. However Bliss wrote several other very worthwhile choral works. These include: *The Golden Cantata* Tenor solo, chorus and orchestra 28 minutes; *Mary of Magdala* Contralto, baritone soli, chorus and orchestra 27 minutes; *The Beatitudes* Soprano, tenor soli, chorus and orchestra 50 minutes

Rutland Boughton

The composer of *The Immortal Hour* needs no reminder as to the effectiveness of his choral writing. His early choral setting *Midnight* for chorus and orchestra (now Boughton Trust, discuss with BMS if interested) 25 minutes is worth consideration. (Boughton was a fine writer for voices, please discuss with BMS if you wish to explore other options by him.)

Alexander Brent Smith

Brent-Smith is largely forgotten as a Three Choirs composer from the interwar years. His *Elegy in Memory of Edward Elgar* for soprano and baritone soli, chorus and orchestra (Novello) 23 minutes is a haunting and powerful piece deserving wide performance.

Sir Herbert Brewer

Emmaus

Soprano, tenor soli, chorus and orchestra (via BMS) ca 40'

Note 6 of the 10 movements of this work are orchestrated by Elgar. (Brewer wrote many choral works for the Three Choirs and a reading of the published vocal scores may suggest other possibilities.)

Samuel Coleridge-Taylor

Meg Blane

Mezzo-sop, chorus and orchestra (via BMS) 30 minutes

A Tale of Old Japan

Soprano, mezzo-soprano, tenor, baritone soli, chorus and orchestra (via BMS) 45 mins

Sir Frederick H Cowen

Cowen was a leading name in British music during the late nineteenth century and many of his choral works were published in vocal score. Many of the full scores of works published by Novello appear not to have survived.

The *Rose Maiden*

SATB soli, chorus and orch (Boosey & Hawkes) 50'

The Transfiguration
SATB soli, chorus and orch (Boosey & Hawkes) 45'

Sir George Dyson
The Sir George Dyson Trust is willing to consider assistance for choirs wishing to programme music by Dyson.

Quo Vadis
SATB soli, chorus and orchestra (Novello) 105 minutes

St Paul's Voyage to Melita
Tenor, chorus and orchestra (Thames) 30 minutes

(There are other approachable choral works by Dyson, ranging in length from *The Canterbury Pilgrims,* a whole evening and now on CD, to the 25-minute *Agincourt.)*

Ernest Farrar
Farrar who was killed towards the end of the First World War was Gerald Finzi's teacher. The full score of his choral setting of Rossetti's *The Blessed Damosel* is lost, but has been re-orchestrated by Rodney Newton.

The Blessed Damosel (re-orchestrated Rodney Newton)
Chorus and orchestra (via BMS) 30 minutes

Herbert Ferrers
Songs of a Roman Legion
Baritone solo, male choir and orchestra (Boosey & Hawkes) 8 miutes

Eric Fogg
Eric Fogg fell under a London tube train in 1939 at the age of 36. He left two choral works both well-received in their day. They were published by Curwen and on the dissolution of that publisher both full scores and performing materials were lost. When the earlier score, *The Hillside,* was revived in 1989, the Broadheath Singers commissioned a re-orchestration from Rodney Newton. This revealed a delightfully fresh and colourful score. (Soprano and baritone soli, chorus and orchestra; materials via BMS) 25 minutes.

John Foulds
In the 1920s *A World Requiem* packed the Albert Hall on Armistices night, but fell out of use and has not been heard complete since 1926. A revival of extracts in 1983 revealed how misleading the vocal score is in trying to assess the music. Novello now have the full score and performing materials, and a revival is long overdue.

(SATB soli, boys' choir, chorus, organ orchestra) about 2 hours.

John Gardner

Gardner has written a variety of popular choral works, among those worth considering are *The Ballad of the White Horse* (Stainer & Bell, 44 mins) and the *Herrick* Cantata.

Cantiones Sacrae
Soprano, chorus and orchestra (Oxford University Press) 45 minutes

C Armstrong Gibbs

Armstrong Gibbs wrote for local choral societies and competitive festivals between the wars. There are many worthwhile choral worth revival, modern performances of *The Highwayman* and *Odysseus* revealed a worthwhile composer of memorable music of wide appeal.)

The *Ballad of Gil Morice*, Op 77
Chorus and orchestra (Boosey & Hawkes) 30 minutes

Deborah and Barak
Contralto and baritone soli, chorus and orchestra (Boosey & Hawkes) 23 minutes

The Highwayman
Chorus and orchestra (Novello) 25 minutes

Odysseus: choral symphony
Soprano and baritone soli, chorus and orchestra (Boosey & Hawkes) 60'

Ruth Gipps
The Cat: cantata
Contralto and baritone soli, chorus and orchestra (Material via BMS) 40 minutes

Sir Eugene Goossens
The Apocalypse
SATB soli, double chorus and orchestra (Boosey & Hawkes) 110'

Patrick Hadley
For those who respond to the idiom of Finzi or Howard Ferguson, choral works by Hadley should be considered. *The Hills* and *The Trees So High* are on CD.

The Hills
Soprano, tenor, baritone Soli, chorus and orchestra (Oxford) 35 minutes

The Travellers
Soprano solo, chorus and orchestra (Oxford) 12 minutes

William Harris
The Hound of Heaven
Baritone, chorus and orchestra (Stainer & Bell) 40 minutes

Julius Harrison
Mass in C
SATB soli, chorus and orchestra (Lengnick) 85 minutes

Psalm 100
chorus and orchestra (Lengnick) ca 15 minutes

Requiem Mass
SATB soli, chorus and orchestra (Lengnick) 60 minutes

The Vision of Cleopatra
Soprano, mezzo-sop, contralto, tenor soli, chorus and orchestra (orchestral parts would need to be written, discuss with BMS) ca 35 minutes

Michael Head
Michael Head is best-known as a song-writer who sang his songs to his own accompaniment. His lyrical gifts are also evident in larger scale works.

Daphne and Apollo
Soprano and baritone soli, chorus and orchestra (Boosey & Hawkes) 25 minutes

George Henschell
Henschell was active as a composer just before Elgar came to fame. His well-turned late Victorian choral music is attractive and published both in vocal score and full score. It may be necessary for any intending performer to write orchestral parts from the printed full scores.

Requiem
SATB soli, chorus and orchestra (Breitkopf) ca 80 minutes

Stabat Mater
SATB soli, chorus and orchestra (Novello)

Tony Hewitt-Jones
Seven Sea Poems
Contralto or baritone solo, chorus and orchestra (Novello) 25 minutes

Te Deum
Contralto, tenor, bass soli, chorus, brass, strings and organ (Boosey & Hawkes)
30 mm

Alun Hoddinott
Hymns of Pantycelyn Op *138*
Baritone, chorus and orchestra (Lengnick) 16 minutes

Gustav Holst
The power of Holst's *Hymn of Jesus* and the appeal of his Choral Symphony
need no special pleading. However Holst wrote a larger catalogue of very
singable choral music. These are some examples of less well-known works

Hymns from the Rig Veda set I
Chorus and orchestra (Stainer & Bell) 14 minutes
(Groups II and IV are for womens' choir and male voice choir respectively)

The Cloud Messenger
Chorus and orchestra (Stainer & Bell) 40 minutes

Gordon Jacob
Highways
Baritone solo, chorus and orchestra (Novello) 40 minutes

John Joubert
Rochester Triptych
Chorus and orchestra (material via BMS) 25 minutes
(This is the glorious work that made such an impact at the 1997 Three Choirs
Festival. There is a significant catalogue of music by Joubert which choral
societies will find worthwhile and enjoyable.)

Liza Lehmann
The Golden Threshold
SATB soli, chorus and orchestra (Boosey & Hawkes) 18 minutes

Sir A C Mackenzie
The orchestral parts of the major choral works by Mackenzie have been lost.
Although the solos from *The Rose of Sharon* were broadcast in 1996, a recent
complete performance was abandoned owing to this problem. For those
wanting to explore Mackenzie performing materials for *The Sun God's Return*
were prepared for a revival in 1993 and are available.

The Rose of Sharon
SATB soli, chorus and orchestra (Novello) 2 hours (or extracts viable)

The Sun God's Return
SATB soli, chorus and orchestra (via BMS) 110 minutes

P Napier Miles
Hymn Before Sunrise
Baritone solo, chorus and orchestra (Boosey & Hawkes) 14 minutes

Bruce Montgomery
Oxford Requiem
Chorus and orchestra (Novello) 20 minutes

Ian Parrott
Psalm 91
Bass solo, chorus and orchestra (Lengnick) 15 minutes

Sir Hubert Parry
Parry's choral works are uneven. Some of his best choral music has now been
revived, and can be heard on Chandos and Hyperion CDs. In particular his
long oratorios need to be approached selectively.

Judith (selections from)
SATB soli, chorus and orchestra (Novello) full work 2″ hours, probably best
heard in Parry's own selection. 35 minutes

Glories of our Blood and State
Chorus and orchestra (Novello) 15 minutes

Montague Phillips
The Death of Admiral Blake (re-orchestrated by William Llewellyn)
Baritone, chorus and orchestra (material via BMS) 19 minutes

Franz Reizenstein
Genesis: an oratorio
Soprano and bass soli, chorus and orchestra (Lengnick) 60 minutes

Cyril B Rootham
Brown Earth
chorus, semi-chorus and orchestra Stainer & Bell) 9 minutes

Ode on the Morning of Christ's Nativity
Soprano and baritone (+ optional extra tenor) soloists, boys choir, chorus and
orchestra
(Stainer & Bell) 50 minutes

Edmund Rubbra
In Die et Nocte Canticum: choral suite
Chorus and orchestra (Lengnick) 18 minutes

The Morning Watch
Chorus and orchestra (Lengnick) 10 minutes
(There are many other worthwhile short choral works by Rubbra, as well as his
choral Ninth Symphony (about 45 minutes). Please consult BMS if interested.)

John Sanders
Gloucestershire Visions
Soprano and tenor soli, chorus and orchestra (via BMS) 25 minutes

Humphrey Searle
Gold Coast Customs (Edith Sitwell)
Speaker, men's chorus and orchestra without strings (Lengnick) 35 minutes
(This powerful piece, one of three by Humphrey Searle with speaker, needs a
strong male voice choir to succeed.)

Matyas Seiber
Ulysses: a cantata after James Joyce
Tenor, chorus and orchestra (Schott) 45 minutes
(For those who have been up to tackling Tippett's A *Child of Our Time* this
would make a rewarding alternative.)

Ethel Smyth
The Prison
Soprano and baritone soli, chorus and orchestra (Novello) ca 60 minutes

Sir Arthur Somervell
Christmas
SATB soli, chorus and orchestra (Boosey & Hawkes) 45 minutes

To the Vanguard
Soprano solo, chorus and orchestra (Boosey & Hawkes) 17 minutes

Sir Charles Villiers Stanford
There are still a large number of occasional works by Stanford well-worth
reviving.

Elegiac Ode
Soprano and baritone soli, chorus and orchestra (Boosey & Hawkes) 25 minutes

Gloria in Exceisis Deo (from *Via Victrix*)
SATB soli, chorus and orchestra (Boosey & Hawkes) 9 minutes
The complete work is well worth considering (60 minutes+) but would need
some work to make ready for performance with orchestra.

The Lord of Might
Chorus and orchestra (Boosey & Hawkes) 10 minutes

Merlin and the Gleam
Baritone, chorus and orchestra ca 35 minutes
(Possibly the finest choral work by Stanford that has not yet been revived.
Please discuss with BMS if wishing to consider, as an orchestration would be
necessary before it could be performed.)

Phaudrig Crohoore: Irish ballad for chorus and orchestra
Chorus and orchestra (Boosey & Hawkes) 15 minutes

Requiem
SATB soli, chorus and orchestra (Boosey & Hawkes) ca 90 minutes
Although recorded on CD (Marco Polo) this fine work is rarely performed
and makes a memorable occasion in the right setting.

The Revenge
Chorus and orchestra (Novello) 23 minutes

Stabat Mater
SATB soli, chorus and orchestra (Boosey & Hawkes) 45 minutes
One of Stanford's finest choral works, recorded on CD. Two of the five
movements are orchestral.

Wellington
Soprano, baritone soli, chorus and orchestra (Boosey & Hawkes) 40 minutes
(Other works by Stanford are worth considering, please discuss with BMS.)

Sir William Sterndale Bennett
Sterndale Bennett's many choral works may now strike some as tame, yet
they are tuneful and beautifully written and have not been heard for many
years. A revival would undoubtedly attract considerable interest.

The May Queen
SATB soli, chorus and orchestra (Boosey & Hawkes) 75 minutes

The Women of Samaria
SATB soli, chorus and orchestra (Boosey & Hawkes) 70 minutes

Sir Arthur Sullivan
On *Shore and Sea: dramatic cantata*
SATB soli, chorus and orchestra (Boosey & Hawkes) 24 minutes
Note: orchestrated by Stanford

The Martyr of Antioch
SATB soli, chorus & orch. (Score and parts from Rev Selwyn Tillett, Librarian, Sir Arthur Sullivan Society, 18 Bloxworth Close, Wallington SM6 7NL) 90mins

Arthur Goring Thomas (orch Stanford)
The Sun and Skylark
SATB soli, chorus and orch (Boosey & Hawkes) 70 minutes

John Veale
Kubla Khan
Baritone, chorus and orchestra (Lengnick) 15 minutes

Sir H Walford Davies
Everyman
(SATB soli, chorus, and orchestra (Novello) 73 minutes

Song of St Francis
SATB soli chorus and orchestra (Novello) ca 60 minutes

R H Walthew
John A-Dreams
SATB soli, chorus and orchestra (Boosey & Hawkes) 27 minutes

Ode to a Nightingale
Bar, chorus and orch (Boosey & Hawkes) 9 minutes

W G Whittaker
A Lyke-Wake Dirge
Chorus and orchestra (via BMS) 12 minutes

Leslie Woodgate
Marginale: six choral pictures
Sop, alto, bass, chorus and orchestra (Boosey & Hawkes) 17 minutes

10. DISCOGRAPHY
OF WORKS PERFORMED

THE FOLLOWING LISTS COMPACT DISC RECORDINGS OF THOSE works heard in the competition which are available in commercially issued recordings.

BERKELEY: *Festival Anthem*
Clare College Choir/Brown/Farr
Meridian CDE 84216

BLACKFORD: *The Mirror of Perfection*
Y Huang, B Skovhus/Bournemouth Symphony Chorus/
Bournemouth Sinfonietta/Richard Blackfoot
Sony Clasical SK 60285

BRIDGE: *A Prayer*
This was recorded with orchestral accompaniment on LP (Chelsea Opera Group Chorus and Orchestra/Williams, Pearl SHE 568). A version with organ accompaniment is on CD:

Vasari Singers, J Backhouse/Filsell
Guild GMCD 7132

BRITTEN: *Cantata Academica*
J Vyvyan, H Watts, P Pears, O Brannigan
London Symphony Choir/LSO/Malcolm
London 436 396-2LM

BRITTEN: *Rejoice in the Lamb*
There are more than a dozen recordings of this in its organ version, including:

Purcell Singers/G Malcolm (org)/Britten
Decca 425 714-2LM

King's College Choir/Ledger
EMI CDM5 65111-2

Westminster Cathedral Choir/Corydon Singers/Best
Hyperion CDA 66126

Finzi Singers/A Lumsden (org)/Spicer
Chandos CHAN 9511

DELIUS: *Songs of Sunset*
O Haley, R Henderson/London Select Choir/LPO/Beecham
(Leeds Festival 1934)
Somm: Beecham 8

M Forrester, J Cameron/Beecham Choral Soc/
RPO/Beecham
EMI CDS7 47509-8

S Burgess, B Terfel/Waynflete Singers/Southern Voices/
Bournemouth Symphony Chorus/Bournemouth SO/Hickox
Chandos CHAN 9214

S Walker, T Allen/Ambrosian Singers/RPO/Fenby Unicorn DKPC 9063

ELGAR: *The Music Makers*
Three surviving extracts of Elgar's own performance in 1927, once on 78s,
appeared on LP and is reissued on CD in The Elgar Edition (EMI CD57
54560-2). Modern recordings include:

J Baker/London Philharmonic Ch/LPO/Boult
EMI CDS7 4708-8

F Palmer/London Sym Ch/LSO/Hickox
EMI CDM5 65126-2; CDC7 47674-2

L Finnie/London Philharmonic Ch/LPO/Thomson
Chandos CHAN 9022

S Walker/BBC Choral Society/BBCSO/del Mar
BBCR 15656 9167-2

J Rigby/BBC Chorus/BBCSO/Davis
Teldec British Line 4509-92374-2

FINZI: *Lo! the Full, Final Sacrifice*
Finzi Singers/H Bicket/Paul Spicer
Chandos CHAN 8936

St Pauls Cathedral Choir/Andrew Lucas (org)/John Scott
Hyperion CDA 66519

FINZI: *Intimations of Immortality*
'Intimations' was first recorded by Vernon Handley on LP but not reissued
on CD (I Patridge/Guildford Philh Choir and Orchestra, Lyrita SRCS 75).

P Langridge/Royal Liverpool Philharmonic Ch/
RLPO/Hickox EMI CDC7 49913-2

J Mark Ainsley/Corydon Singers/Corydon Orch/Best
Hyperion CDA 66876

PARRY: *Blest Pair of Sirens*
Sir Adrian Boult first recorded 'Blest Pair' on two 78rpm discs (Oxford Bach
Choir/LSO HMV HMV C 3820-1). Modern recordings include:

London Philharmonic Choir/LPO/Boult
EMI CDC 7 49022-2; CDM 565107-2

London Philharmonic Choir/LPO/Boult
AS Disc AS 534
(Sir Adrian Boult 80th Birthday Concert 8/4/69)

PARRY: *Ode on the Nativity*
Not issued on CD but was once recorded on LP which has not been reissued
(T Cahill/Bach Choir/RCM Chorus/LPO/Willcocks, Lyrita SRCS 125).

RUBBRA: *Song of the Soul* (1952)
Academy of St Martin in the Fields Chorus/
City of London Sinfonia/Richard Hickox.
Chandos CHAN 9847

RUTTER: *Psalmfest* (1973-94)
Psalmfest consists of nine movements for varied forces. The work has not
been commercially recorded complete, but six of its nine movements are on
various CDs as follows. All are by the New Cambridge Singers/City of London
Sinfonia/Rutter unless otherwise stated.

No 1: 'O be joyful in the Lord'
  Collegium COLCD 112
No 2: 'I will lift up mine eyes'
  Collegium COLCD 103
No 4: 'The Lord is my shepherd'
  Collegium COLCD 100
No 5: 'Cantate Domino'
  Bournemouth Polyphony/Layton Hyperion CDA 66947
No 7: 'O clap your hands'
  Collegium COLCD 100
No 9: 'O praise the Lord of heaven'
  Collegium COLCD 114

SULLIVAN: *The Golden Legend*
M Wild, J Watson, J Rigby, J Black/
London Chorus/New London Orch/ Ronald Corp
Hyperion CDA 67280

SULLIVAN: *Te Deum Laudamus* (*Festival Te Deum*, 1872)
The only recording of this score was issued as a cover-mounted CD with *BBC Music Magazine* Vol 9 No 7 (March 2001) and is available as a back-issue (T Cahill, London Choral Society, BBC Concert Orch/M Phillips (org)/ Ronald Corp)

VAUGHAN WILLIAMS: *Toward the Unknown Region*
London Symphony Orchestra Chorus/LSO/Sargent
EMI CDM 7 63382

Waynflete Singers/Winchester Cathedral Choir/
Bournemouth SO/Hill
Argo 436 120-2ZH

London Symphony Choir/LSO/Thomson
Chandos CHAN 8796; 9262/3

City of Birmingham Symphony Orchestra Choir/CBSO/del Mar
EMI CDM5 65131-2

Corydon Singers/Corydon Orch/Best Hyperion CDA 66655

EDITOR'S ACKNOWLEDGEMENTS

MANY HAVE CONTRIBUTED TO MAKE THIS PUBLICATION A REALITY and I would like to thank all who have been involved. First, all the contributors, and particularly the authors of the various programme notes which appeared during the Millennium Choral Competition and which are reprinted here. To them thanks for permission to reprint them here; they remain the copyright of the individual contributors. To Roger Carpenter who masterminded its passage through the printer, and to Garry Humphreys who read the text in proof and made many helpful suggestions. Also to the officials and Musical Directors of the participating choirs who patiently answered many queries for the reference section. Finally to all who were involved in organising and running the BMS Millennium Choral Competition and in particular Stan Meares without whose organisational flair it would never have happened.